The Chronicles of Froissart

Translated by

John Bourchier

(Lord Berners)

Cover: *The Battle of Crecy*, from an early manuscript of Froissart's Chronicles, Bibliothèque Nationale de France

ISBN: 978-1-78139-023-8

Printed on acid free ANSI archival quality paper.

© 2011 Benediction Classics, Oxford.

Contents

Introduction 1

Chapter 1 The Campaign of Crecy 5

How the King of England came over the sea again, to rescue them in Aiguillon 7

How the King of England rode in three battles through Normandy 10

Of the great assembly that the French King made to resist the King of England 13

Of the Battle of Caen, and how the Englishmen took the town 16

How Sir Godfrey of Harcourt fought with them of Amiens before Paris 19

How the French King followed the King of England in Beauvoisinois 23

Of the Battle of Blanche-Taque between the King of England and Sir Godemar du Fay 26

Of the order of the Englishmen at Cressy, and how they made three battles afoot 30

The Order of the Frenchmen at Cressy, and how they beheld the demeanour of the Englishmen 32

Of the Battle of Cressy between the King of England and the French King 34

How the next day after the Battle the Englishmen discomfited divers Frenchmen 40

How the next day after the Battle of Cressy they that were dead were numbered by the Englishmen 42

Chapter 2 The Battle of Poitiers 45

Of the great host that the French King brought to the Battle of Poitiers 47

Of the order of the Frenchmen before the Battle of Poitiers .. 51

How the Cardinal of Perigord treated to make agreement between the French King and the Prince before the Battle of Poitiers 54

Of the Battle of Poitiers between the Prince of Wales and the French King 59

Of two Frenchmen that fled from the Battle of Poitiers and two Englishmen that followed them 67

How King John was taken prisoner at the Battle of Poitiers . 69

Of the gift that the Prince gave to the Lord Audley after the Battle of Poitiers 73

How the Englishmen won greatly at the Battle of Poitiers 75

How the Lord James Audley gave to his four squires the five hundred marks of revenues that the Prince had given him 77

How the Prince made a supper to the French King the same day of the battle 79

How the Prince returned to Bordeaux after the Battle of Poitiers 80

Chapter 3 Wat Tyler's Rebellion 85

How the Commons of England rebelled against the Noblemen 87

The evil deeds that these Commons of England did to the King's Officers, and how they sent a knight to speak with the King 92

How the Commons of England entered into London, and of the great evil that they did, and of the death of the Bishop of Canterbury and divers others 97

How the nobles of England were in great peril to have been destroyed, and how these rebels were punished and sent home to their own houses 102

Chapter 4 The Battle of Otterburn 113

How the Earl Douglas won the pennon of Sir Henry Percy at the barriers before Newcastle-upon-Tyne, and how the Scots brent the Castle of Pontland, and how Sir Henry Percy and Sir Ralph his Brother took advice to follow the Scots to conquer again the pennon that was lost at the scrimmish 115

How Sir Henry Percy and his brother with a good number of men of arms and archers went after the Scots, to win again his pennon that the Earl Douglas had won before Newcastle-upon-Tyne, and how they assailed the Scots before Otterburn in their lodgings 120

How the Earl James Douglas by his valiantness encouraged his men, who were reculed and in a manner discomfited, and in his so doing he was wounded to death..............................124

How in this Battle Sir Ralph Percy was sore hurt and taken prisoner by a Scottish knight..126

How the Scots won the Battle against the Englishmen beside Otterburn, and there was taken prisoners Sir Henry and Sir Ralph Percy, and how an English squire would not yield him, no more would a Scottish squire, and so died both; and how the Bishop of Durham and his company were discomfited among themselves 129

How Sir Matthew Redman departed from the Battle to save himself; and how Sir James Lindsay was taken prisoner by the Bishop of Durham; and how after the Battle scurrers were sent forth to discover the country 134

How the Scots departed and carried with them the Earl Douglas dead, and buried him in the Abbey of Melrose; and how Sir Archambault Douglas and his company departed from before Carlisle and returned into Scotland...................140

Index **145**

Introduction

JEAN FROISSART, the most representative of the chroniclers of the later Middle Ages, was born at Valenciennes in 1337. The Chronicle which, more than his poetry, has kept his fame alive, was undertaken when he was only twenty; the first book was written in its earliest form by 1369; and he kept revising and enlarging the work to the end of his life. In 1361 he went to England, entered the Church, and attached himself to Queen Philippa of Hainault, the wife of Edward III, who made him her secretary and clerk of her chapel. Much of his life was spent in travel. He went to France with the Black Prince, and to Italy with the Duke of Clarence. He saw fighting on the Scottish border, visited Holland, Savoy, and Provence, returning at intervals to Paris and London. He was Vicar of Estinnes-au-Mont, Canon of Chimay, and chaplain to the Comte de Blois; but the Church to him was rather a source of revenue than a religious calling. He finally settled down in his native town, where he died about 1410.

Froissart's wandering life points to one of the most prominent of his characteristics as a historian. Uncritical and often inconsistent as he is, his mistakes are not due to Partisanship, for he is extraordinarily cosmopolitan. The Germans he dislikes as unchivalrous; but though his life lay in the period of the Hundred Years' War between England and France, and though he describes many of the events of that war, he is as friendly to England as to France.

By birth Froissart belonged to the bourgeoisie, but his tastes and associations made him an aristocrat. Glimpses of the sufferings which the lower classes underwent in the wars of his time appear in his pages, but they are given incidentally and without sympathy. His interests are all in the somewhat degenerate chivalry of his age, in the splendour of courts, the pomp and circumstance of war, in tourneys, and in pageantry. Full of the love of adventure, he would travel across half of Europe to see a gallant feat of arms, a coronation, a royal marriage. Strength and courage and loyalty were the virtues he loved; cowardice and petty greed he hated. Cruelty and injustice could not dim for him the brilliance of the careers of those brigand lords who were his friends and patrons.

The material for the earlier part of his Chronicles he took largely from his predecessor and model, Jean Lebel; the later books are filled with narratives of what he saw with his own eyes, or gathered from the lips of men who had themselves been part of what they told. This fact, along with his mastery of a style which is always vivacious if sometimes diffuse, accounts for the vividness and picturesqueness of his work. The Pageant of medieval life in court and camp dazzled and delighted him, and it is as a Pageant that we see the Middle Ages in his book.

Froissart holds a distinguished place among the poets as well as the historians of his century. He wrote chiefly in the allegorical style then in vogue; and his poems, though cast in a mould no longer in fashion, are fresh and full of colour, and were found worthy of imitation by Geoffrey Chaucer.

But it is as the supreme chronicler of the later age of chivalry that he lives. "God has been gracious enough," he writes, "to permit me to visit the courts and palaces of kings, . . . and all the nobles, kings, dukes, counts, barons, and knights, belonging to all nations, have been kind to me, have listened to me, willingly received me, and proved very useful to me. . . . Wherever I went I enquired of old knights and squires who had

Introduction

shared in deeds of arms, and could speak with authority concerning them, and also spoke with heralds in order to verify and corroborate all that was told me. In this way I gathered noble facts for my history, and as long as I live, I shall, by the grace of God, continue to do this, for the more I labour at this the more pleasure I have, and I trust that the gentle knight who loves arms will be nourished on such noble fare, and accomplish still more."

G. C. MACAULAY
1910

Chapter 1
The Campaign of Crecy

How the King of England came over the sea again, to rescue them in Aiguillon

THE king of England, who had heard how his men were sore constrained in the castle of Aiguillon, then he thought to go over the sea into Gascoyne with a great army. There he made his provision and sent for men all about his realm and in other places, where he thought to speed for his money. In the same season the lord Godfrey of Harcourt came into England, who was banished out of France: he was well received with the king and retained to be about him, and had fair lands assigned him in England to maintain his degree. Then the king caused a great navy of ships to be ready in the haven of Hampton, and caused all manner of men of war to draw thither. About the feast of Saint John Baptist the year of our Lord God MCCCXLVI., the king departed from the queen and left her in the guiding of the earl of Kent his cousin; and he stablished the lord Percy and the lord Nevill to be wardens of his realm with [the archbishop of Canterbury,] the archbishop of York, the bishop of Lincoln and the bishop of Durham; for he never voided his realm but that he left ever enough at home to keep and defend the realm, if need were. Then the king rode to Hampton and there tarried for wind: then he entered into his ship and the prince of Wales with him, and the lord Godfrey of Harcourt, and all other lords, earls, barons and knights, with all their companies. They were in number a four thousand men of arms and ten thousand archers, beside Irishmen and Welshmen that followed the host afoot.

Now I shall name you certain of the lords that went over with king Edward in that journey. First, Edward his eldest son, prince of Wales, who as then was of the age of thirteen years or thereabout,* the earls of Hereford, Northampton, Arundel, Cornwall, Warwick, Huntingdon, Suffolk, and Oxford; and of barons the lord Mortimer, who was after earl of March, the lords John, Louis and Roger of Beauchamp, and the lord Raynold Cobham; of lords the lord of Mowbray, Ros, Lucy, Felton, Bradestan, Multon, Delaware, Manne,† Basset, Berkeley, and Willoughby, with divers other lords; and of bachelors there was John Chandos, Fitz-Warin, Peter and James Audley, Roger of Wetenhale, Bartholomew of Burghersh, and Richard of Pembridge, with divers other that I cannot name. Few there were of strangers‡: there was the earl Hainault,§ It means, 'of the county of Hainault, there was sir Wulfart of Ghistelles, and five or six other knights of Almaine, and many other that I cannot name.

Thus they sailed forth that day in the name of God. They were well onward on their way toward Gascoyne, but on the third day there rose a contrary wind and drave them on the marches of Cornwall, and there they lay at anchor six days. In that space the king had other counsel by the means of sir Godfrey Harcourt: he counselled the king not to go into Gascoyne, but rather to set aland in Normandy, and said to the king: 'Sir, the country of Normandy is one of the plenteous countries of the world: sir, on jeopardy of my head, if ye will land there, there is none that shall resist you; the people of Normandy have not been used to the War, and all the knights and squires of the country are now at the siege before Aiguillon with the duke. And, sir, there ye shall find great towns that be not walled, whereby your men shall have such winning, that they shall be the better thereby twenty year after; and, sir, ye may

---

* He was in fact sixteen; born 15th June 1330.
† Probably 'Mohun.'
‡ stranger = foreigner
§ The usual confusion between 'comte' and 'comte.'

follow with your army till ye come to Caen in Normandy: sir, I require you to believe me in this voyage.'

The king, who was as then but in the flower of his youth, desiring nothing so much as to have deeds of arms, inclined greatly to the saying of the lord Harcourt, whom he called cousin. Then he commanded the mariners to set their course to Normandy, and he took into his ship the token of the admiral the earl of Warwick, and said how he would be admiral for that viage, and so sailed on before as governour of that navy, and they had wind at will. Then the king arrived in the isle of Cotentin, at a port called Hogue Saint-Vaast.[**]

Tidings anon spread abroad how the Englishmen were aland: the towns of Cotentin sent word thereof to Paris to king Philip. He had well heard before how the king of England was on the sea with a great army, but he wist not what way he would draw, other into Normandy, Bretayne or Gascoyne. As soon as he knew that the king of England was aland in Normandy, he sent his constable the earl of Guines, and the earl of Tancarville, who were but newly come to him from his son from the siege at Aiguillon, to the town of Caen, commanding them to keep that town against the Englishmen. They said they would do their best: they departed from Paris with a good number of men of war, and daily there came more to them by the way, and so came to the town of Caen, where they were received with great joy of men of the town and of the country thereabout, that were drawn thither for surety. These lords took heed for the provision of the town, the which as then was not walled. The king thus was arrived at the port Hogue Saint-Vaast near to Saint-Saviour the Viscount [††] the right heritage to the lord Godfrey of Harcourt, who as then was there with the king of England.

[**] Saint-Vaast-de la Hogue.
[††] Saint-Sauveur-le-Vicomte.

9

How the King of England rode in three battles through Normandy

WHEN the king of England arrived in the Hogue Saint-Vaast, the king issued out of his ship, and the first foot that he set on the ground, he fell so rudely, that the blood brast* out of his nose. The knights that were about him took him up and said: 'Sir, for God's sake enter again into your ship, and come not aland this day, for this is but an evil sign for us.' Then the king answered quickly and said: 'Wherefore? This is a good token for me, for the land desireth to have me.' Of the which answer all his men were right joyful. So that day and night the king lodged on the sands, and in the meantime discharged the ships of their horses and other baggages: there the king made two marshals of his host, the one the lord Godfrey of Harcourt and the other the earl of Warwick, and the earl of Arundel constable. And he ordained that the earl of Huntingdon should keep the fleet of ships with a hundred men of arms and four hundred archers: and also he ordained three battles, one to go on his right hand, closing to the sea-side, and the other on his left hand, and the king himself in the midst, and every night to lodge all in one field.

Thus they set forth as they were ordained, and they that went by the sea took all the ships that they found in their ways: and so long they went forth, what by sea and what by land, that they came to a good port and to a good town called Barfleur, the

---

* brast = burst.

which incontinent was won, for they within gave up for fear of death. Howbeit, for all that, the town was robbed, and much gold and silver there found, and rich jewels: there was found so much riches, that the boys and villains of the host set nothing by good furred gowns: they made all the men of the town to issue out and to go into the ships, because they would not suffer them to be behind them for fear of rebelling again. After the town of Barfleur was thus taken and robbed without brenning[†], then they spread abroad in the country and did what they list, for there was not to resist them. At last they came to a great and a rich town called Cherbourg: the town they won and robbed it, and brent part thereof, but into the castle they could not come, it was so strong and well furnished with men of war. Then they passed forth and came to Montebourg, and took it and robbed and brent it clean. In this manner they brent many other towns in that country and won so much riches, that it was marvel to reckon it. Then they came to a great town well closed called Carentan, where there was also a strong castle and many soldiers within to keep it. Then the lords came out of their ships and fiercely made assault: the burgesses of the town were in great fear of their lives, wives and children: they suffered the Englishmen to enter into the town against the will of all the soldiers that were there; they put all their goods to the Englishmen's pleasures, they thought that most advantage. When the soldiers within saw that, they went into the castle: the Englishmen went into the town, and two days together they made sore assaults, so that when they within saw no succour, they yielded up, their lives and goods saved, and so departed. The Englishmen had their pleasure of that good town and castle, and when they saw they might not maintain to keep it, they set fire therein and brent it, and made the burgesses of the town to enter into their ships, as they had done with them of Barfleur, Cherbourg and Montebourg, and of other towns that they had won on the sea-side. All this was done

---

[†] bren = burn

by the battle that went by the sea-side, and by them on the sea together. ‡

Now let us speak of the king's battle. When he had sent his first battle along by the sea-side, as ye have heard, whereof one of his marshals, the earl of Warwick, was captain, and the lord Cobham with him, then he made his other marshal to lead his host on his left hand, for he knew the issues and entries of Normandy better than any other did there. The lord Godfrey as marshal rode forth with five hundred men of arms, and rode off from the king's battle as six or seven leagues, in brenning and exiling the country, the which was plentiful of everything -- the granges full of corn, the houses full of all riches, rich burgesses, carts and chariots, horse, swine, muttons and other beasts: they took what them list and brought into the king's host; but the soldiers made no count to the king nor to none of his officers of the gold and silver that they did get; they kept that to themselves. Thus sir Godfrey of Harcourt rode every day off from the king's host, and for most part every night resorted to the king's field. The king took his way to Saint-Lo in Cotentin, but or he came there he lodged by a river, abiding for his men that rode along by the sea-side; and when they were come, they set forth their carriage, and the earl of Warwick, the earl of Suffolk, sir Thomas Holland and sir Raynold Cobham, and their company rode out on the one side and wasted and exiled the country, as the lord Harcourt had done; and the king ever rode between these battles, and every night they lodged together.

---

‡ Froissart is mistaken in supposing that a division of the land army went to these towns: Barfleur and Cherbourg were visited only by the fleet. According to Michael of Northburgh, who accompanied the expedition, Edward disembarked 12th July and remained at Saint-Vaast till the 18th, and meanwhile the fleet went to Barfleur and Cherbourg. The army arrived at Caen on the 26th.

Of the great assembly that the French King made to resist the King of England

THUS by the Englishmen was brent, exiled, robbed, wasted and pilled the good, plentiful country of Normandy. Then the French king sent for the lord John of Hainault, who came to him with a great number: also the king sent for other men of arms, dukes, earls, barons, knights and squires, and assembled together the greatest number of people that had been seen in France a hundred year before. He sent for men into so far countries, that it was long or they came together, wherefore the king of England did what him list in the mean season. The French king heard well what he did, and sware and said how they should never return again unfought withal, and that such hurts and damages as they had done should be dearly revenged; wherefore he had sent letters to his friends in the Empire, to such as were farthest off, and also to the gentle king of Bohemia and to the lord Charles his son, who from thenceforth was called king of Almaine; he was made king by the aid of his father and the French king, and had taken on him the arms of the Empire: the French king desired them to come to him with all their powers, to the intent to fight with the king of England, who brent and wasted his country. These princes and lords made them ready with great number of men of arms, of Almains, Bohemians and Luxemburgers, and so came to the French king. Also king Philip sent to the duke of Lorraine, who came to serve him with three hundred spears: also there came the earl [of] Salm in Saumois, the earl of Sarrebruck, the earl of Flanders, the earl William of Namur, every man with a fair company.

Ye have heard herebefore of the order of the Englishmen, how they went in three battles, the marshals on the right hand and on the left, the king and the prince of Wales his son in the midst. They rode but small journeys and every day took their lodgings between noon and three of the clock, and found the country so fruitful, that they needed not to make no provision for their host, but all only for wine; and yet they found reasonably sufficient thereof.[*] It was no marvel though they of the country were afraid, for before that time they had never seen men of war, nor they wist not what war or battle meant. They fled away as far as they might hear speaking of the Englishmen,[†] and left their houses well stuffed, and granges full of corn, they wist not how to save and keep it. The king of England and the prince had in their battle a three thousand men of arms and six thousand archers and a ten thousand men afoot, beside them that rode with the marshals.

Thus as ye have heard, the king rode forth, wasting and brenning the country without breaking of his order. He left the city of Coutances[‡] and went to a great town called Saint-Lo, a rich town of drapery and many rich burgesses. In that town there were dwelling an eight or nine score burgesses, crafty men. When the king came there, he took his lodging without, for he would never lodge in the town for fear of fire: but he sent his men before and anon the town was taken and clean robbed. It was hard to think the great riches that there was won, in clothes

---

[*] Or rather, 'thus they found reasonably sufficient provisions.'

[†] That is, they fled as soon as they heard their coming spoken of.

[‡] That is, he did not turn aside to go to it. Froissart says, 'He did not turn aside to the city of Coutances, but went on toward the great town of Saint-Loin Cotentin, which at that time was very rich and of great merchandise and three times as great as the city of Coutances.' Michael of Northburgh says that Barfleur was about equal in importance to Sandwich and Carentan to Leicester, Saint-Lo greater than Lincoln, and Caen greater than any city in England except London.

specially; cloth would there have been sold good cheap, if there had been any buyers.

Then the king went toward Caen, the which was a greater town and full of drapery and other merchandise, and rich burgesses, noble ladies and damosels, and fair churches, and specially two great and rich abbeys, one of the Trinity, another of Saint Stephen; and on the one side of the town one of the fairest castles of all Normandy, and captain therein was Robert of Wargny, with three hundred Genoways, and in the town was the earl of Eu and of Guines, constable of France, and the earl of Tancarville, with a good number of men of war. The king of England rode that day in good order and lodged all his battles together that night, a two leagues from Caen, in a town with a little haven called Austrehem, and thither came also all his navy of ships with the earl of Huntingdon, who was governour of them.

The constable and other lords of France that night watched well the town of Caen, and in the morning armed them with all them of the town: then the constable ordained that none should issue out, but keep their defences on the walls, gate, bridge and river, and left the suburbs void because they were not closed; for they thought they should have enough to do to defend the town, because it was not closed but with the river. They of the town said how they would issue out, for they were strong enough to fight with the king of England. When the constable saw their good wills, he said: 'In the name of God be it, ye shall not fight without me.' Then they issued out in good order and made good face to fight and to defend them and to put their lives in adventure.

Of the Battle of Caen, and how the Englishmen took the town

THE same day the Englishmen rose early and apparelled them ready to go to Caen.* The king heard mass before the sun-rising and then took his horse, and the prince his son, with sir Godfrey of Harcourt marshal and leader of the host, whose counsel the king much followed. Then they drew toward Caen with their battles in good array, and so approached the good town of Caen. When they of the town, who were ready in the field, saw these three battles coming in good order, with their banners and standards waving in the wind, and the archers, the which they had not been accustomed to see, they were sore afraid and fled away toward the town without any order or good array, for all that the constable could do: then the Englishmen pursued them eagerly. When the constable and the earl Tancarville saw that, they took a gate at the entry and saved themselves† and certain with them, for the Englishmen were entered into the town. Some of the knights and squires of France, such as knew the way to the castle, went thither, and the captain there received them all, for the castle was large. The Englishmen in the chase slew many, for they took none to mercy.

---

* This was 26th July. Edward arrived at Poissy On 12th August: Philip of Valois left Paris on the 14th: the English crossed the Seine at Poissy on the 16th and the Somme at Blanche-taque on the 24th.

† 'Set themselves for safety in a gate at the entry of the bridge.'

The Campaign of Crecy

Then the constable and the earl of Tancarville, being in the little tower at the bridge foot, looked along the street and saw their men slain without mercy: they doubted to fall in their hands. At last they saw an English knight with one eye called sir Thomas Holland, and a five or six other knights with him: they knew them, for they had seen them before in Pruce, in Granade, and in other viages. Then they called to sir Thomas and said how they would yield themselves prisoners. Then sir Thomas came thither with his company and mounted up into the gate, and there found the said lords with twenty-five knights with them, who yielded them to sir Thomas, and he took them for his prisoners and left company to keep them, and then mounted again on his horse and rode into the streets, and saved many lives of ladies, damosels, and cloisterers from defoiling, for the soldiers were without mercy. It fell so well the same season for the Englishmen, that the river, which was able to bear ships, at that time was so low, that men went in and out beside the bridge. They of the town were entered into their houses, and cast down into the street stones, timber and iron, and slew and hurt more than five hundred Englishmen, wherewith the king was sore displeased. At night when he heard thereof, he commanded that the next day all should be put to the sword and the town brent; but then sir Godfrey of Harcourt said: 'Dear sir, for God's sake assuage somewhat your courage, and let it suffice you that ye have done. Ye have yet a great voyage to do or ye come before Calais, whither ye purpose to go; and, sir, in this town there is much people who will defend their houses, and it will cost many of your men their lives, or ye have all at your will; whereby peradventure ye shall not keep your purpose to Calais, the which should redound to your rack. Sir, save your people, for ye shall have need of them or this month pass; for I think verily your adversary king Philip will meet with you to fight, and ye shall find many straight passages and rencounters; wherefore your men, an ye had more, shall stand you in good stead: and, sir, without any further slaying ye shall be lord of this town; men and women will put all that they have to your pleasure.' Then the king said: 'Sir Godfrey, you are our marshal, ordain everything as ye will.' Then sir Godfrey with his banner rode from street to street, and commanded in the king's name none to be so hardy to put fire in any house, to slay any person, nor to violate any woman. When they of the town heard that cry, they received the Englishmen into their houses and made them good cheer, and some opened their coffers and bade them take what them list, so they might be assured of their lives; howbeit there were done in the town many evil deeds, murders and robberies. Thus the Englishmen were lords of the town three days and won great riches, the which they sent by barks and barges to Saint-Saviour by the river of Austrehem[‡], a two leagues thence, whereas all their navy lay. Then the king sent the earl of Huntingdon with two hundred men of arms and four hundred archers, with his navy and prisoners and riches that they had got, back again into England. And the king bought of sir Thomas Holland the constable of France and the earl of Tancarville, and paid for them twenty thousand nobles.

[‡] Froissart says that they sent their booty in barges and boats 'on the river as far as Austrehem, a two leagues from thence, where their great navy lay.' He makes no mention of Saint-Sauveur here. The river in question is the Orne, at the mouth of which Austrehem is situated.

How Sir Godfrey of Harcourt fought with them of Amiens before Paris

THUS the king of England ordered his business, being in the town of Caen, and sent into England his navy of ships charged with clothes, jewels, vessels of gold and silver, and of other riches, and of prisoners more than sixty knights and three hundred burgesses. Then he departed from the town of Caen and rode in the same order as he did before, brenning and exiling the country, and took the way to Evreux and so passed by it; and from thence they rode to a great town called Louviers: it was the chief town of all Normandy of drapery, riches, and full of merchandise. The Englishmen soon entered therein, for as then it was not closed; it was overrun, spoiled and robbed without mercy: there was won great riches. Then they entered into the country of Evreux and brent and pilled all the country except the good towns closed and castles, to the which the king made none assault, because of the sparing of his people and his artillery.

On the river of Seine near to Rouen there was the earl of Harcourt, brother to sir Godfrey of Harcourt, but he was on the French party, and the earl of Dreux with him, with a good number of men of war: but the Englishmen left Rouen and went to Gisors, where was a strong castle: they brent the town and then they brent Vernon and all the country about Rouen and Pont-de-l'Arche and came to Mantes and to Meulan, and wasted all the country about, and passed by the strong castle of Rolleboise; and in every place along the river of Seine they found the bridges broken. At last they came to Poissy, and found the bridge broken, but the arches and joists lay in the river: the king lay there a five days: in the mean season the bridge was made, to pass the host without peril. The English marshals ran abroad just to Paris, and brent Saint-Germain in Laye and Montjoie, and Saint-Cloud, and petty Boulogne by Paris, and the Queen's Bourg:* they of Paris were not well assured of themselves, for it was not as then closed.

Then king Philip removed to Saint-Denis, and or he went caused all the pentices† in Paris to be pulled down; and at Saint-Denis were ready come the king of Bohemia, the lord John of Hainault, the duke of Lorraine, the earl of Flanders, the earl of Blois, and many other great lords and knights, ready to serve the French king. When the people of Paris saw their king depart, they came to him and kneeled down and said: 'Ah, sir and noble king, what will ye do? leave thus this noble city of Paris?' The king said: 'My good people, doubt ye not: the Englishmen will approach you no nearer than they be.' 'Why so, sir?' quoth they; 'they be within these two leagues, and as soon as they know of your departing, they will come and assail us; and we not able to defend them: sir, tarry here still and help to defend your good city of Paris.' 'Speak no more,' quoth the king, 'for I will go to Saint-Denis to my men of war: for I will encounter the Englishmen and fight against them, whatsoever fall thereof.'

The king of England was at Poissy, and lay in the nunnery there, and kept there the feast of our Lady in August and sat in his robes of scarlet furred with ermines; and after that feast he went forth in order as they were before. The lord Godfrey of Harcourt rode out on the one side with five hundred men of arms and thirteen‡ hundred archers; and by adventure he encountered a great number of burgesses of Amiens a-

---

* Bourg-la-Reine.

† pentice = an extension of a building's roof and the protected area beneath.

‡ A better reading is 'twelve.'

horseback, who were riding by the king's commandment to Paris. They were quickly assailed and they defended themselves valiantly, for they were a great number and well armed: there were four knights of Amiens their captains. This skirmish dured long: at the first meeting many were overthrown on both parts; but finally the burgesses were taken and nigh all slain, and the Englishmen took all their carriages and harness. They were well stuffed, for they were going to the French king well appointed, because they had not seen him a great season before. There were slain in the field a twelve hundred.

Then the king of England entered into the country of Beauvoisis, brenning and exiling the plain country, and lodged at a fair abbey and a rich called Saint-Messie§ near to Beauvais: there the king tarried a night and in the morning departed. And when he was on his way he looked behind him and saw the abbey a-fire: he caused incontinent twenty of them to be hanged that set the fire there, for he had commanded before on pain of death none to violate any church nor to bren any abbey. Then the king passed by the city of Beauvais without any assault giving, for because he would not trouble his people nor waste his artillery. And so that day he took his lodging betime in a little town called Milly. The two marshals came so near to Beauvais, that they made assault and skirmish at the barriers in three places, the which assault endured a long space; but the town within was so well defended by the means of the bishop, who was there within, that finally the Englishmen departed, and brent clean hard to the gates all the suburbs, and then at night they came into the king's field.

The next day the king departed, brenning and wasting all before him, and at night lodged in a good village called Grandvilliers. The next day the king passed by Dargies: there was none to defend the castle, wherefore it was soon taken and

---

§ Commonly called Saint-Lucien, but Saint-Maximianus (Messien) is also associated with the place.

brent. Then they went forth destroying the country all about, and so came to the castle of Poix, where there was a good town and two castles. There was nobody in them but two fair damosels, daughters to the lord of Poix; they were soon taken, and had been violated, an two English knights had not been, sir John Chandos and sir Basset; they defended them and brought them to the king, who for his honour made them good cheer and demanded of them whither they would fainest go. They said, 'To Corbie,' and the king caused them to be brought thither without peril. That night the king lodged in the town of Poix. They of the town and of the castles spake that night with the marshals of the host, to save them and their town from brenning, and they to pay a certain sum of florins the next day as soon as the host was departed. This was granted them, and in the morning the king departed with all his host except a certain that were left there to receive the money that they of the town had promised to pay. When they of the town saw the host depart and but a few left behind, then they said they would pay never a penny, and so ran out and set on the Englishmen, who defended themselves as well as they might and sent after the host for succour. When sir Raynold Cobham and sir Thomas Holland, who had the rule of the rearguard, heard thereof, they returned and cried, 'Treason, treason!' and so came again to Poix-ward and found their companions still fighting with them of the town. Then anon they of the town were nigh all slain, and the town brent, and the two castles beaten down. Then they returned to the king's host, who was as then at Airaines and there lodged, and had commanded all manner of men on pain of death to do no hurt to no town of Arsyn,[**] for there the king was minded to lie a day or two to take advice how he might pass the river of Somme; for it was necessary for him to pass the river, as ye shall hear after.

[**] A mistranslation. The original is '(il avoit) defendu sus le hart que nuis ne fourfesist rien a le ville d'arin ne d'autre cose,' 'he had commanded all on pain of hanging to do no hurt to the town by burning or otherwise.' The translator has taken 'arsin' for a proper name.

How the French King followed the King of England in Beauvoisinois

Now let us speak of King Philip, who was at Sant-Denis and his people about him, and daily increased. Then on a day he departed and rode so long that he came to Coppegueule, a three leagues from Amiens, and there he tarried. The king of England being at Airaines wist not where for to pass the river of Somme, the which was large and deep, and all bridges were broken and the passages well kept. Then at the king's commandment his two marshals with a thousand men of arms and two thousand archers went along the river to find some passage, and passed by Longpre, and came to the bridge of Remy,* the which was well kept with a great number of knights and squires and men of the country. The Englishmen alighted afoot and assailed the Frenchmen from the morning till it was noon; but the bridge was so well fortified and defended, that the Englishmen departed without winning of anything. Then they went to a great town called Fountains on the river of Somme, the which was clean robbed and brent, for it was not closed. Then they went to another town called Long-en-Ponthieu; they could not win the bridge, it was so well kept and defended. Then they departed and went to Picquigny, and found the town, the bridge, and the castle so well fortified, that it was not likely to pass there: the French king had so well defended the passages, to the intent that the king of England should not pass the river of Somme, to fight with him at his advantage or else to famish him there.

---

* Pont-a-Remy, corrupted here into 'bridge of Athyne.'

When these two marshals had assayed in all places to find passage and could find none, they returned again to the king, and shewed how they could find no passage in no place. The same night the French king came to Amiens with more than a hundred thousand men. The king of England was right pensive, and the next morning heard mass before the sun-rising and then dislodged; and every man followed the marshals' banners and so rode in the country of Vimeu approaching to the good town of Abbeville, and found a town thereby, whereunto was come much people of the country in trust of a little defence that was there; but the Englishmen anon won it, and all they that were within slain, and many taken of the town and of the country. The king took his lodging in a great hospital[†] The same day the French king departed from Amiens and came to Airaines about noon; and the Englishmen were departed thence in the morning. The Frenchmen found there great provision that the Englishmen had left behind them, because they departed in haste. There they found flesh ready on the broaches, bread and pasties in the ovens, wine in tuns and barrels, and the tables ready laid. There the French king lodged and tarried for his lords.

That night the king of England was lodged at Oisemont. At night when the two marshals were returned, who had that day overrun the country to the gates of Abbeville and to Saint-Valery and made a great skirmish there, then the king assembled together his council and made to be brought before him certain prisoners of the country of Ponthieu and of Vimeu. The king right courteously demanded of them, if there were any among them that knew any passage beneath Abbeville, that he and his host might pass over the river of Somme: if he would shew him thereof, he should be quit of his ransom, and twenty of his company for his love. There was a varlet called Gobin Agace who stepped forth and said to the king: 'Sir, I promise you on the jeopardy of my head I shall bring you to such a place, whereas ye and all your host shall pass the river of Somme

---

[†] That is, a house of the knights of Saint John. that was there.

without peril. There be certain places in the passage that ye shall pass twelve men afront two times between day and night: ye shall not go in the water to the knees. But when the flood cometh, the river then waxeth so great, that no man can pass; but when the flood is gone, the which is two times between day and night, then the river is so low, that it may be passed without danger both a-horseback and afoot. The passage is hard in the bottom with white stones, so that all your carriage may go surely; therefore the passage is called Blanche-taque. An ye make ready to depart betimes, ye may be there by the sun-rising.' The king said: 'If this be true that ye say, I quit thee thy ransom and all thy company, and moreover shall give thee a hundred nobles.' Then the king commanded every man to be ready at the sound of the trumpet to depart.

Of the Battle of Blanche-Taque between the King of England and Sir Godemar du Fay

THE king of England slept not much that night, for at midnight he arose and sowned his trumpet: then incontinent they made ready carriages and all things, and at the breaking of the day they departed from the town of Oisemont and rode after the guiding of Gobin Agace, so that they came by the sun-rising to Blanche-taque; but as then the flood was up, so that they might not pass: so the king tarried there till it was prime; then the ebb came.

The French king had his currours[*] in the country, who brought him word of the demeanour of the Englishmen. Then he thought to close the king of England between Abbeville and the river of Somme, and so to fight with him at his pleasure. And when he was at Amiens he had ordained a great baron of Normandy, called sir Godemar du Fay, to go and keep the passage of Blanche-taque, where the Englishmen must pass or else in none other place. He had with him a thousand men of arms and six thousand afoot, with the Genoways: so they went by Saint-Riquier in Ponthieu and from thence to Crotoy, whereas the passage lay; and also he had with him a great number of men of the country, and also a great number of them of Montreuil, so that they were a twelve thousand men one and other.

---

[*] currours = light cavalrymen

When the English host was come thither, sir Godemar du Fay arranged all his company to defend the passage. The king of England let not for all that; but when the flood was gone, he commanded his marshals to enter into the water in the name of God and Saint George. Then they that were hardy and courageous entered on both parties, and many a man reversed. There were some of the Frenchmen of Artois and Picardy that were as glad to joust in the water as on the dry land.

The Frenchmen defended so well the passage at the issuing out of the water, that they had much to do. The Genoways did them great trouble with their cross-bows: on the other side the archers of England shot so wholly together, that the Frenchmen were fain to give place to the Englishmen. There was a sore battle, and many a noble feat of arms done on both sides. Finally the Englishmen passed over and assembled together in the field. The king and the prince passed, and all the lords; then the Frenchmen kept none array, but departed, he that might best. When sir Godemar saw that discomfiture, he fled and saved himself: some fled to Abbeville and some to Saint-Riquiers. They that were there afoot could not flee, so that there were slain a great number of them of Abbeville, Montreuil, Rue and of Saint-Riquiers: the chase endured more than a great league. And as yet all the Englishmen were not passed the river, and certain currours of the king of Bohemia and of sir John of Hainault came on them that were behind and took certain horses and carriages and slew divers, or they could take the passage.

The French king the same morning was departed from Airaines, trusting to have found the Englishmen between him and the river of Somme: but when he heard how that sir Godemar du Fay and his company were discomfited, he tarried in the field and demanded of his marshals what was best to do. They said, 'Sir, ye cannot pass the river but at the bridge of Abbeville, for the flood is come in at Blanche-taque': then he returned and lodged at Abbeville.

The king of England when he was past the river, he thanked God and so rode forth in like manner as he did before. Then he called Gobin Agace and did quit him his ransom and all his company, and gave him a hundred nobles and a good horse. And so the king rode forth fair and easily, and thought to have lodged in a great town called Noyelles; but when he knew that the town pertained to the countess d'Aumale, sister to the lord Robert of Artois,[†] the king assured the town and country as much as pertained to her, and so went forth; and his marshals rode to Crotoy on the sea-side and brent the town, and found in the haven many ships and barks charged with wines of Poitou, pertaining to the merchants of Saintonge and of Rochelle: they brought the best thereof to the king's host. Then one of the marshals rode to the gates of Abbeville and from thence to Saint-Riquiers, and after to the town of Rue-Saint-Esprit. This was on a Friday, and both battles of the marshals returned to the king's host about noon and so lodged all together near to Cressy in Ponthieu.

The king of England was well informed how the French king followed after him to fight. Then he said to his company: 'Let us take here some plot of ground, for we will go no farther till we have seen our enemies. I have good cause here to abide them, for I am on the right heritage of the queen my mother, the which land was given at her marriage: I will challenge it of mine adversary Philip of Valois.' And because that he had not the eighth part in number of men as the French king had, therefore he commanded his marshals to chose a plot of ground somewhat for his advantage: and so they did, and thither the king and his host went. Then he sent his currours to Abbeville, to see if the French king drew that day into the field or not. They went forth and returned again, and said how they could see none appearance of his coming: then every man took their lodging for that day, and to be ready in the morning at the sound of the trumpet in the same place. This Friday the French king tarried

---

[†] She was in fact his daughter.

The Campaign of Crecy

still in Abbeville abiding for his company, and sent his two marshals to ride out to see the dealing of the Englishmen, and at night they returned, and said how the Englishmen were lodged in the fields. That night the French king made a supper to all the chief lords that were there with him, and after supper the king desired them to be friends each to other. The king looked for the earl of Savoy, who should come to him with a thousand spears, for he had received wages for a three months of them at Troyes in Champagne.

Of the order of the Englishmen at Cressy, and how they made three battles afoot

ON the Friday, as I said before, the king of England lay in the fields, for the country was plentiful of wines and other victual, and if need had been, they had provision following in carts and other carriages. That night the king made a supper to all his chief lords of his host and made them good cheer; and when they were all departed to take their rest, then the king entered into his oratory and kneeled down before the altar, praying God devoutly, that if he fought the next day, that he might achieve the journey to his honour: then about midnight he laid him down to rest, and in the morning he rose betimes and heard mass, and the prince his son with him, and the most part of his company were confessed and houselled[*]; and after the mass said, he commanded every man to be armed and to draw to the field to the same place before appointed. Then the king caused a park to be made by the wood side behind his host, and there was set all carts and carriages, and within the park were all their horses, for every man was afoot; and into this park there was but one entry. Then he ordained three battles: in the first was the young prince of Wales, with him the earl of Warwick and Oxford, the lord Godfrey of Harcourt, sir Raynold Cobham, sir Thomas Holland, the lord Stafford, the lord of Mohun, the lord Delaware, sir John Chandos, sir Bartholomew de Burghersh, sir Robert Nevill, the lord Thomas Clifford, the lord Bourchier, the lord de Latimer, and divers other knights and squires that I cannot name: they were an eight hundred men of arms and two

---

[*] housel = to administer the Eucharist to.

The Campaign of Crecy

thousand archers, and a thousand of other with the Welshmen: every lord drew to the field appointed under his own banner and pennon. In the second battle was the earl of Northampton, the earl of Arundel, the lord Ros, the lord Lucy, the lord Willoughby, the lord Basset, the lord of Saint-Aubin, sir Louis Tufton, the lord of Multon, the lord Lascelles and divers other, about an eight hundred men of arms and twelve hundred archers. The third battle had the king: he had seven hundred men of arms and two thousand archers. Then the king leapt on a hobby,[†] with a white rod in his hand, one of his marshals on the one hand and the other on the other hand: he rode from rank to rank desiring every man to take heed that day to his right and honour. He spake it so sweetly and with so good countenance and merry cheer, that all such as were discomfited took courage in the seeing and hearing of him. And when he had thus visited all his battles, it was then nine of the day: then he caused every man to eat and drink a little, and so they did at their leisure. And afterward they ordered again their battles: then every man lay down on the earth and by him his salet[‡] and bow, to be the more fresher when their enemies should come.

[†] 'Un petit palefroi.'
[‡] salet = a helmet.

The Order of the Frenchmen at Cressy, and how they beheld the demeanour of the Englishmen

THIS Saturday the French king rose betimes and heard mass in Abbeville in his lodging in the abbey of Saint Peter, and he departed after the sun-rising. When he was out of the town two leagues, approaching toward his enemies, some of his lords said to him: 'Sir, it were good that ye ordered your battles, and let all your footmen pass somewhat on before, that they be not troubled with the horsemen.' Then the king sent four knights, the Moine [of] Bazeilles, the lord of Noyers, the lord of Beaujeu and the lord d'Aubigny to ride to aview the English host; and so they rode so near that they might well see part of their dealing. The Englishmen saw them well and knew well how they were come thither to aview them: they let them alone and made no countenance toward them, and let them return as they came. And when the French king saw these four knights return again, he tarried till they came to him and said: 'Sirs, what tidings?' These four knights each of them looked on other, for there was none would speak before his companion; finally the king said to [the] Moine, who pertained to the king of Bohemia and had done in his days so much, that he was reputed for one of the valiantest knights of the world: 'Sir, speak you.' Then he said: 'Sir, I shall speak, sith it pleaseth you, under the correction of my fellows. Sir, we have ridden and seen the behaving of your enemies: know ye for truth they are rested in three battles abiding for you. Sir, I will counsel you as for my part, saving your displeasure, that you and all your company rest here and lodge for this night: for or they that be behind of your company be come hither, and or your battles be set in good order, it will be very late, and your people be weary and out of array, and ye shall find your enemies fresh and ready to receive you. Early in the morning ye may order your battles at more leisure and advise your enemies at more deliberation, and to regard well what way ye will assail them; for, sir, surely they will abide you.'

Then the king commanded that it should be so done. Then his two marshals one rode before, another behind, saying to every banner: 'Tarry and abide here in the name of God and Saint Denis.' They that were foremost tarried, but they that were behind would not tarry, but rode forth, and said how they would in no wise abide till they were as far forward as the foremost: and when they before saw them come on behind, then they rode forward again, so that the king nor his marshals could not rule them. So they rode without order or good array, till they came in sight of their enemies: and as soon as the foremost saw them, they reculed[*] then aback without good array, whereof they behind had marvel and were abashed, and thought that the foremost company had been fighting. Then they might have had leisure and room to have gone forward, if they had list: some went forth and some abode still. The commons, of whom all the ways between Abbeville and Cressy were full, when they saw that they were near to their enemies, they took their swords and cried: 'Down with them! let us slay them all.' There is no man, though he were present at the journey, that could imagine or shew the truth of the evil order that was among the French party, and yet they were a marvellous great number. That I write in this book I learned it specially of the Englishmen, who well beheld their dealing; and also certain knights of sir John of Hainault's, who was always about king Philip, shewed me as they knew.

---

[*] recule = recoil, retreat

Of the Battle of Cressy between the King of England and the French King

THE Englishmen, who were in three battles lying on the ground to rest them, as soon as they saw the Frenchmen approach, they rose upon their feet fair and easily without any haste and arranged their battles. The first, which was the prince's battle, the archers there stood in manner of a herse* and the men of arms in the bottom of the battle. The earl of Northampton and the earl of Arundel with the second battle were on a wing in good order, ready to comfort the prince's battle, if need were.

The lords and knights of France came not to the assembly together in good order, for some came before and some came after in such haste and evil order, that one of them did trouble another. When the French king saw the Englishmen, his blood changed, and said to his marshals: 'Make the Genoways go on before and begin the battle in the name of God and Saint Denis.' There were of the Genoways cross-bows about a fifteen thousand,† but they were so weary of going afoot that day a six leagues armed with their cross-bows, that they said to their constables: 'We be not well ordered to fight this day, for we be not in the case to do any great deed of arms: we have more need of rest.' These words came to the earl of Alencon ,

---

* herse = harrow, possibly here in the sense of a set of spikes set into a frame, laid in the path of enemy cavalry.
† Villani, a very good authority on the subject, says 6000, brought from the ships at Harfleur.

who said: 'A man is well at ease to be charged with such a sort of rascals, to be faint and fail now at most need.' Also the same season there fell a great rain and a clipse[‡] with a terrible thunder, and before the rain there came flying over both battles a great number of crows for fear of the tempest coming. Then anon the air began to wax clear, and the sun to shine fair and bright, the which was right in the Frenchmen's eyen and on the Englishmen's backs. When the Genoways were assembled together and began to approach, they made a great leap[§] and cry to abash the Englishmen, but they stood still and stirred not for all that: then the Genoways again the second time made another leap and a fell cry, and stept forward a little, and the Englishmen removed not one foot: thirdly, again they leapt and cried, and went forth till they came within shot; then they shot fiercely with their cross-bows. Then the English archers stept forth one pace and let fly their arrows so wholly [together] and so thick, that it seemed snow. When the Genoways felt the arrows piercing through heads, arms and breasts, many of them cast down their cross-bows and did cut their strings and returned discomfited. When the French king saw them fly away, he said: 'Slay these rascals, for they shall let and trouble us without reason.' Then ye should have seen the men of arms dash in among them and killed a great number of them: and ever still the Englishmen shot whereas they saw thickest press; the sharp arrows ran into the men of arms and into their horses, and many fell, horse and men, among the Genoways, and when they were down, they could not

---

[‡] A mistranslation of 'une esclistre,' 'a flash of lightning.'

[§] These 'leaps' of the Genoese are invented by the translator, and have passed from him into several respectable English text-books, sometimes in company with the eclipse above mentioned. Froissart says: 'Il commencierent a juper mouit epouvantablement'; that is, 'to utter cries.' Another text makes mention of the English cannons at this point: 'The English remained still and let off some cannons that they had, to frighten the Genoese.'

relieve[**] again, the press was so thick that one overthrew another. And also among the Englishmen there were certain rascals that went afoot with great knives, and they went in among the men of arms, and slew and murdered many as they lay on the ground, both earls, barons, knights and squires, whereof the king of England was after displeased, for he had rather they had been taken prisoners.

The valiant king of Bohemia called Charles[††] of Luxembourg, son to the noble emperor Henry of Luxembourg, for all that he was nigh blind, when he understood the order of the battle, he said to them about him: 'Where is the lord Charles my son?' His men said: 'Sir, we cannot tell; we think he be fighting.' Then he said: 'Sirs, ye are my men, my companions and friends in this journey: I require you bring me so far forward, that I may strike one stroke with my sword.' They said they would do his commandment, and to the intent that they should not lose him in the press, they tied all their reins of their bridles each to other and set the king before to accomplish his desire, and so they went on their enemies. The lord Charles of Bohemia his son, who wrote himself king of Almaine and bare the arms, he came in good order to the battle; but when he saw that the matter went awry on their party, he departed, I cannot tell you which way. The king his father was so far forward that he strake a stroke with his sword, yea and more than four, and fought valiantly and so did his company; and they adventured themselves so forward, that they were there all slain, and the next day they were found in the place about the king, and all their horses tied each to other.

The earl of Alencon came to the battle right ordinately and fought with the Englishmen, and the earl of Flanders also on

---

[**] The translator's word 'relieve' (relyuue) represents 'relever,' for 'se relever.'
[††] Should be John, not Charles

his part. These two lords with their companies coasted the English archers and came to the prince's battle, and there fought valiantly long. The French king would fain have come thither, when he saw their banners, but there was a great hedge of archers before him. The same day the French king had given a great black courser to sir John of Hainault, and he made the lord Tierry of Senzeille to ride on him and to bear his banner. The same horse took the bridle in the teeth and brought him through all the currours of the Englishmen, and as he would have returned again, he fell in a great dike and was sore hurt, and had been there dead, an his page had not been, who followed him through all the battles and saw where his master lay in the dike, and had none other let but for his horse, for the Englishmen would not issue out of their battle for taking of any prisoner. Then the page alighted and relieved his master: then he went not back again the same way that they came, there was too many in his way.

This battle between Broye and Cressy this Saturday was right cruel and fell, and many a feat of arms done that came not to my knowledge. In the night‡‡ divers knights and squires lost their masters, and sometime came on the Englishmen, who received them in such wise that they were ever nigh slain; for there was none taken to mercy nor to ransom, for so the Englishmen were determined.

In the morning§§ [of] the day of the battle certain Frenchmen and Almains perforce opened the archers of the prince's battle and came and fought with the men of arms hand to hand. Then the second battle of the Englishmen came to

---

‡‡ 'Sus le nuit,' 'towards nightfall.'

§§ The text has suffered by omissions. What Froissart says is that if the battle had begun in the morning, it might have gone better for the French, and then he instances the exploits of those who broke through the archers. The battle did not begin till four o'clock in the afternoon.

succour the prince's battle, the which was time, for they had as then much ado; and they with the prince sent a messenger to the king, who was on a little windmill hill. Then the knight said to the king: 'Sir, the earl of Warwick and the earl of Oxford, sir Raynold Cobham and other, such as be about the prince, your son, are fiercely fought withal and are sore handled; wherefore they desire you that you and your battle will come and aid them; for if the Frenchmen increase, as they doubt they will, your son and they shall have much ado.' Then the king said: 'Is my son dead or hurt or on the earth felled?' 'No, sir,' quoth the knight, 'but he is hardly matched; wherefore he hath need of your aid.' 'Well' said the king, 'return to him and to them that sent you hither, and say to them that they send no more to me for any adventure that falleth, as long as my son is alive: and also say to them that they suffer him this day to win his spurs;*** for if God be pleased, I will this journey be his and the honour thereof, and to them that be about him.' Then the knight returned again to them and shewed the king's words, the which greatly encouraged them, and repoined††† in that they had sent to the king as they did.

Sir Godfrey of Harcourt would gladly that the earl of Harcourt his brother might have been saved; for he heard say by them that saw his banner how that he was there in the field on the French party: but sir Godfrey could not come to him betimes, for he was slain or he could come at him, and so was also the earl of Aumale his nephew. In another place the earl of Alencon and the earl of Flanders fought valiantly, every lord under his own banner; but finally they could not resist against the puissance of the Englishmen, and so there they were also slain, and divers other knights and squires. Also the earl Louis of Blois, nephew to the French king, and the duke of Lorraine fought under their banners, but at last they were closed in among

---

*** 'Que il laissent a l'enfant gaegnier ses esperons.'

††† i.e. 'they repoined': Fr. 'se reprisent.'

The Campaign of Crecy

a company of Englishmen and Welshmen, and there were slain for all their prowess. Also there was slain the earl of Auxerre, the earl of Saint-Pol and many other.

In the evening the French king, who had left about him no more than a three-score persons, one and other, whereof sir John of Hainault was one, who had remounted once the king, for his horse was slain with an arrow, then he said to the king: 'Sir, depart hence, for it is time; lose not yourself wilfully: if ye have loss at this time, ye shall recover it again another season.' And so he took the king's horse by the bridle and led him away in a manner perforce. Then the king rode till he came to the castle of Broye. The gate was closed, because it was by that time dark: then the king called the captain, who came to the walls and said: 'Who is that calleth there this time of night?' Then the king said: 'Open your gate quickly, for this is the fortune of France.[‡‡‡] The captain knew then it was the king, and opened the gate and let down the bridge. Then the king entered, and he had with him but five barons, sir John of Hainault, sir Charles of Montmorency, the lord of Beaujeu, the lord d'Aubigny and the lord of Montsault. The king would not tarry there, but drank and departed thence about midnight, and so rode by such guides as knew the country till he came in the morning to Amiens, and there he rested.

This Saturday the Englishmen never departed from their battles for chasing of any man, but kept still their field, and ever defended themselves against all such as came to assail them. This battle ended about evensong time.

[‡‡‡] 'C'est la fortune de France': but the better MSS. have 'c'est li infortunes rois de France.'

How the next day after the Battle the Englishmen discomfited divers Frenchmen

ON this Saturday, when the night was come and that the Englishmen heard no more noise of the Frenchmen, then they reputed themselves to have the victory, and the Frenchmen to be discomfited, slain and fled away. Then they made great fires and lighted up torches and candles, because it was very dark. Then the king avaled* down from the little hill whereas he stood; and of all that day till then his helm came never on his head. Then he went with all his battle to his son the prince and embraced him in his arms and kissed him, and said: 'Fair son, God give you good perseverance; ye are my good son, thus ye have acquitted you nobly: ye are worthy to keep a realm.' The prince inclined himself to the earth, honouring the king his father.

This night they thanked God for their good adventure and made no boast thereof, for the king would that no man should be proud or make boast, but every man humbly to thank God. On the Sunday in the morning there was such a mist, that a man might not see the breadth of an acre of land from him. Then there departed from the host by the commandment of the king and marshals five hundred spears and two thousand archers, to see if they might see any Frenchmen gathered again together in any place. The same morning out of Abbeville and Saint-Riquiers in Ponthieu the commons of Rouen and of Beauvais issued out of their towns, not knowing of the discomfiture of the

---

* avale = descend.

day before. They met with the Englishmen weening[†] they had been Frenchmen, and when the Englishmen saw them, they set on them freshly, and there was a sore battle; but at last the Frenchmen fled and kept none array. There were slain in the ways and in hedges and bushes more than seven thousand and if the day had been clear there had never a one escaped. Anon after, another company of Frenchmen were met by the Englishmen, the archbishop of Rouen and the great prior of France, who also knew nothing of the discomfiture the day before; for they heard that the French king should have fought the same Sunday, and they were going thitherward. When they met with the Englishmen, there was a great battle, for they were a great number, but they could not endure against the Englishmen; for they were nigh all slain, few escaped; the two lords were slain. This morning the Englishmen met with divers Frenchmen that had lost their way on the Saturday and had lain all night in the fields, and wist not where the king was nor the captains. They were all slain, as many as were met with; and it was shewed me that of the commons and men afoot of the cities and good towns of France there was slain four times as many as were slain the Saturday in the great battle.

[†] ween = believe.

How the next day after the Battle of Cressy they that were dead were numbered by the Englishmen

THE same Sunday, as the king of England came from mass, such as had been sent forth returned and shewed the king what they had seen and done, and said: 'Sir, we think surely there is now no more appearance of any of our enemies.' Then the king sent to search how many were slain and what they were. Sir Raynold Cobham and sir Richard Stafford with three heralds went to search the field and country: they visited all them that were slain and rode all day in the fields, and returned again to the host as the king was going to supper. They made just report of that they had seen, and said how there were eleven great princes dead, fourscore banners, twelve hundred knights, and more than thirty thousand other.[*] The Englishmen kept still their field all that night: on the Monday in the morning the king prepared to depart: the king caused the dead bodies of the great lords to be taken up and conveyed to Montreuil, and there buried in holy ground, and made a cry in the country to grant truce for three days, to the intent that they of the country might search the field of Cressy to bury the dead bodies.

---

[*] Another text makes the loss of persons below the rank of knight 15,000 or 16,000, including the men of the towns. Both estimates must be greatly exaggerated. Michael of Northburgh says that 1542 were killed in the battle and about 2000 on the next day. The great princes killed were the king of Bohemia, the duke of Lorraine, the earls of Alencon, Flanders, Blois, Auxerre, Harcourt, Saint-Pol, Aumale, the grand prior of France and the archbishop of Rouen.

The Campaign of Crecy

Then the king went forth and came before the town of Montreuil-by-the-sea, and his marshals ran toward Hesdin and brent Waben and Serain, but they did nothing to the castle, it was so strong and so well kept. They lodged that night on the river of Hesdin towards Blangy. The next day they rode toward Boulogne and came to the town of Wissant: there the king and the prince lodged, and tarried there a day to refresh his men, and on the Wednesday the king came before the strong town of Calais.

Chapter 2
The Battle of Poitiers

Of the great host that the French King brought to the Battle of Poitiers

AFTER the taking of the castle of Romorantin and of them that were therein, the prince then and his company rode as they did before, destroying the country, approaching to Anjou and to Touraine. The French king , who was at Chartres, departed and came to Blois and there tarried two days, and then to Amboise and the next day to Loches: and then he heard how that the prince was at Touraine[*] and how that he was returning by Poitou: ever the Englishmen were coasted by certain expert knights of France, who alway made report to the king what the Englishmen did. Then the king came to the Haye in Touraine and his men had passed the river of Loire, some at the bridge of Orleans and some at Meung, at Saumur, at Blois, and at Tours and whereas they might: they were in number a twenty thousand men of arms beside other; there were a twenty-six dukes and earls and more than sixscore banners, and the four sons of the king, who were but young, the duke Charles of Normandy, the lord Louis, that was from thenceforth duke of Anjou, and the lord John duke of Berry, and the lord Philip, who was after duke of Burgoyne. The same season, pope Innocent the sixth sent the lord Bertrand, cardinal of Perigord, and the lord Nicholas, cardinal of Urgel, into France, to treat for a peace between the French king and all his enemies, first between him and the king of Navarre, who was in prison: and these cardinals oftentimes spake to the king for his deliverance during the siege at Bretuel, but they could do nothing in that behalf. Then the cardinal of

---

[*] "En Touraine."

Perigord went to Tours, and there he heard how the French king hasted sore to find the Englishmen: then he rode to Poitiers, for he heard how both the hosts drew thitherward.

The French king heard how the prince hasted greatly to return, and the king feared that he should scape him and so departed from Haye in Touraine, and all his company, and rode to Chauvigny, where he tarried that Thursday in the town and without along by the river of Creuse, and the next day the king passed the river at the bridge there, weening that the Englishmen had been before him, but they were not. Howbeit they pursued after and passed the bridge that day more than threescore thousand horses, and divers other passed at Chatelleraut, and ever as they passed they took the way to Poitiers.

On the other side the prince wist not truly where the Frenchmen were; but they supposed that they were not far off, for they could not find no more forage, whereby they had great fault in their host of victual, and some of them repented that they had destroyed so much as they had done before when they were in Berry, Anjou and Touraine, and in that they had made no better provision. The same Friday three great lords of France, the lord of Craon, the lord Raoul of Coucy and the earl of Joigny, tarried all day at the town of Chauvigny, and part of their companies. The Saturday they passed the bridge and followed the king, who was then a three leagues before, and took the way among bushes without a wood side to go to Poitiers.

The same Saturday the prince and his company dislodged from a little village thereby, and sent before him certain currours to see if they might find any adventure and to hear where the Frenchmen were. They were in number a three-score men of arms well horsed, and with them was the lord Eustace d'Aubrecicourt and the lord John of Ghistelles, and by adventure the Englishmen and Frenchmen met together by the foresaid wood side. The Frenchmen knew anon how they were their enemies; then in haste they did on their helmets and displayed

The Battle of Poitiers

their banners and came a great pace towards the Englishmen: they were in number a two hundred men of arms. When the Englishmen saw them, and that they were so great a number, then they determined to fly and let the Frenchmen chase them, for they knew well the prince with his host was not far behind. Then they turned their horses and took the corner of the wood, and the Frenchmen after them crying their cries and made great noise. And as they chased, they came on the prince's battle or they were ware thereof themselves; the prince tarried there to have word again from them that he sent forth. The lord Raoul de Coucy with his banner went so far forward that he was under the prince's banner: there was a sore battle and the knight fought valiantly; howbeit he was there taken, and the earl of Joigny, the viscount of Brosse, the lord of Chauvigny and all the other taken or slain, but a few that scaped. And by the prisoners the prince knew how the French king followed him in such wise that he could not eschew the battle:[†] then he assembled together all his men and commanded that no man should go before the marshals' banners. Thus the prince rode that Saturday from the morning till it was against night, so that he came within two little leagues of Poitiers. Then the captal[‡] de Buch, sir Aymenion of Pommiers, the lord Bartholomew of Burghersh and the lord Eustace d'Aubrecicourt, all these the prince sent forth to see if they might know what the Frenchmen did. These knights departed with two hundred men of arms well horsed: they rode so far that they saw the great battle of the king's, they saw all the fields covered with men of arms. These Englishmen could not forbear, but set on the tail of the French host and cast down many to the earth and took divers prisoners, so that the host began to stir, and tidings thereof came to the French king as he was entering into the city of Poitiers. Then he returned again and

---

[†] Or rather, 'that the French king had gone in front of them (les avoit avancez) and that he could in no way depart without being fought with.'

[‡] captal = chief, from Latin capitalis.

made all his host do the same, so that Saturday it was very late or he was lodged in the field. The English currours returned again to the prince and shewed him all that they saw and knew, and said how the French host was a great number of people. 'Well,' said the prince, 'in the name of God let us now study how we shall fight with them at our advantage.' That night the Englishmen lodged in a strong place among hedges, vines and bushes, and their host well watched, and so was the French host.

Of the order of the Frenchmen before the Battle of Poitiers

ON the Sunday in the morning the French king, who had great desire to fight with the Englishmen, heard his mass in his pavilion and was houselled, and his four sons with him. After mass there came to him the duke of Orleans, the duke of Bourbon, the earl of Ponthieu, the lord Jaques of Bourbon,* the duke of Athens, constable of France, the earl of Tancarville, the earl of Sarrebruck, the earl of Dammartin, the earl of Ventadour, and divers other great barons of France and of other neighbours holding of France, as the lord Clermont, the lord Arnold d'Audrehem, marshal of France, the lord of Saint-Venant, the lord John of Landas, the lord Eustace Ribemont, the lord Fiennes, the lord Geoffrey of Charny, the lord Chatillon, the lord of Sully, the lord of Nesle, sir Robert Duras and divers other; all these with the king went to counsel. Then finally it was ordained that all manner of men should draw into the field, and every lord to display his banner and to set forth in the name of God and Saint Denis: then trumpets blew up through the host and every man mounted on horseback and went into the field, where they saw the king's banner wave with the wind. There might a been seen great nobles of fair harness and rich armoury of banners and pennons; for there was all the flower of France, there was none durst abide at home without he would be shamed for ever. Then it was ordained by the advice of the constable and marshals to be made three battles, and in each ward sixteen thousand men of arms all mustered and passed for men of arms. The first battle

---

* That is, Jaques de Bourbon, earl of la Marche and Ponthieu.

the duke of Orleans to govern, with thirty-six banners and twice as many pennons, the second the duke of Normandy and his two brethren the lord Louis and the lord John, the third the king himself: and while that these battles were setting in array, the king called to him the lord Eustace Ribemont, the lord John of Landas and the lord Richard of Beaujeu, and said to them: 'Sirs, ride on before to see the dealing of the Englishmen and advise well what number they be and by what means we may fight with them, other afoot or a-horseback.' These three knights rode forth and the king was on a white courser and said a-high to his men: 'Sirs, among you, when ye be at Paris, at Chartres, at Rouen or at Orleans, then ye do threat the Englishmen and desire to be in arms out against them. Now ye be come thereto: I shall now shew you them: now shew forth your evil will that ye bear them and revenge your displeasures and damages that they have done you, for without doubt we shall fight with them.' Such as heard him said: 'Sir, in God's name so be it; that would we see[†] gladly.'

Therewith the three knights returned again to the king, who demanded of them tidings. Then sir Eustace of Ribemont answered for all and said: 'Sir, we have seen the Englishmen: by estimation they be two thousand men of arms and four thousand archers and a fifteen hundred of other. Howbeit they be in a strong place, and as far as we can imagine they are in one battle; howbeit they be wisely ordered, and along the way they have fortified strongly the hedges and bushes: one part of their archers are along by the hedge, so that none can go nor ride that way, but must pass by them, and that way must ye go an ye purpose to fight with them. In this hedge there is but one entry and one issue by likelihood that four horsemen may ride afront. At the end of this hedge, whereas no man can go nor ride, there be men of arms afoot and archers afore them in manner of a herse, so

---

[†] 'Verrons': but a better reading is 'ferons,' 'that will we do gladly.'

The Battle of Poitiers

that they will not be lightly discomfited.'[‡] In this hedge there is but one entry and one issue, where by likelihood four men of arms, as on the road, might ride a-front. At the end of this hedge among vines and thorn-bushes, where no man can go nor ride, are their men of arms all afoot, and they have set in front of them their archers in manner of a harrow, whom it would not be easy to discomfit. 'Well,' said the king, 'what will ye then counsel us to do?' Sir Eustace said: 'Sir, let us all be afoot, except three hundred men of arms, well horsed, of the best in your host and most hardiest, to the intent they somewhat to break and to open the archers, and then your battles to follow on quickly afoot and so to fight with their men of arms hand to hand. This is the best advice that I can give you: if any other think any other way better, let him speak.' The king said: 'Thus shall it be done': then the two marshals rode from battle to battle and chose out a three hundred knights and squires of the most expert men of arms of all the host, every man well armed and horsed. Also it was ordained that the battles of Almains should abide still on horseback to comfort the marshals, if need were, whereof the earl of Sarrebruck, the earl of Nidau and the earl of Nassau were captains. King John of France was there armed, and twenty other in his apparel; and he did put the guiding of his eldest son to the lord of Saint-Venant, the lord of Landas and the lord Thibault of Vaudenay; and the lord Arnold of Cervolles, called the archpriest,[§] was armed in the armour of the young earl of Alencon.

[‡] The translation of this passage is unsatisfactory. It should be: 'Howbeit they have ordered it wisely, and have taken post along the road, which on one side (or according to another text, on one side and on the other) with their archers, so that one cannot enter nor ride along their road except by them, and that way must he go who purposes to fight with them.

[§] Arnaud de Cervolles, one of the most celebrated adventurers of the 14th century, called the archpriest because though a layman he possessed the ecclesiastical fief of Velines.

How the Cardinal of Perigord treated to make agreement between the French King and the Prince before the Battle of Poitiers

WHEN the French king's battles was ordered and every lord under his banner among their own men, then it was commanded that every man should cut their spears to a five foot long and every man to put off their spurs. Thus as they were ready to approach, the cardinal of Perigord[*] came in great haste to the king. He came the same morning from Poitiers; he kneeled down to the king and held up his hands and desired him for God's sake a little to abstain setting forward till he had spoken with him: then he said: 'Sir, ye have here all the flower of your realm against a handful of Englishmen as to regard your company,[†] and, sir, if ye may have them accorded to you without battle, it shall be more profitable and honourable to have them by that manner rather than to adventure so noble chivalry as ye have here present. Sir, I require you in the name of God and humility that I may ride to the prince and shew him what danger ye have him in.' The king said: 'It pleaseth me well, but return again shortly.' The cardinal departed and diligently he rode to the prince, who was among his men afoot: then the cardinal alighted and came to the prince, who received him courteously. Then the cardinal after his salutation made he said: 'Certainly,

---

[*] Talleyrand de Perigord.

[†] The meaning is, 'Ye have here all the flower of your realm against a handful of people, for so the Englishmen are as compared with your company.'

The Battle of Poitiers

fair son, if you and your council advise justly the puissance of the French king, ye will suffer me to treat to make a peace between you, an I may.' The prince, who was young and lusty, said: 'Sir, the honour of me and of my people saved, I would gladly fall to any reasonable way.' Then the cardinal said: 'Sir, ye say well, and I shall accord you, an I can; for it should be great pity if so many noblemen and other as be here on both parties should come together by battle.' Then the cardinal rode again to the king and said: 'Sir, ye need not to make any great haste to fight with your enemies, for they cannot fly from you though they would, they be in such a ground: wherefore, sir, I require you forbear for this day till tomorrow the sun-rising.' The king was loath to agree thereto, for some of his council would not consent to it; but finally the cardinal shewed such reasons, that the king accorded that respite: and in the same place there was pight‡ up a pavilion of red silk fresh and rich, and gave leave for that day every man to draw to their lodgings except the constable's and marshals' battles.

That Sunday all the day the cardinal travailed in riding from the one host to the other gladly to agree them: but the French king would not agree without he might have four of the principallest of the Englishmen at his pleasure, and the prince and all the other to yield themselves simply: howbeit there were many great offers made. The prince offered to render into the king's hands all that ever he had won in that voyage, towns and castles, and to quit all prisoners that he or any of his men had taken in that season, and also to swear not to be armed against the French king in seven year after; but the king and his council would none thereof: the uttermost that he would do was, that the prince and a hundred of his knights should yield themselves into the king's prison; otherwise he would not: the which the prince would in no wise agree unto.

---

‡ pight = pitch.

In the mean season that the cardinal rode thus between the hosts in trust to do some good, certain knights of France and of England both rode forth the same Sunday, because it was truce for that day, to coast the hosts and to behold the dealing of their enemies. So it fortuned that the lord John Chandos rode the same day coasting the French host, and in like manner the lord of Clermont, one of the French marshals, had ridden forth and aviewed the state of the English host; and as these two knights returned towards their hosts, they met together: each of them bare one manner of device, a blue lady embroidered in a sunbeam above on their apparel. Then the lord Clermont said: 'Chandos, how long have ye taken on you to bear my device?' 'Nay, ye bear mine,' said Chandos, 'for it is as well mine as yours.' 'I deny that,' said Clermont, 'but an it were not for the truce this day between us, I should make it good on you incontinent that ye have no right to bear my device.' 'Ah, sir,' said Chandos, 'ye shall find me to-morrow ready to defend you and to prove by feat of arms that it is as well mine as yours.' Then Clermont said: 'Chandos, these be well the words of you Englishmen, for ye can devise nothing of new, but all that ye see is good and fair.' So they departed without any more doing, and each of them returned to their host.

The cardinal of Perigord could in no wise that Sunday make any agreement between the parties, and when it was near night he returned to Poitiers. That night the Frenchmen took their ease; they had provision enough, and the Englishmen had great default; they could get no forage, nor they could not depart thence without danger of their enemies. That Sunday the Englishmen made great dikes and hedges about their archers, to be the more stronger; and on the Monday in the morning the prince and his company were ready apparelled as they were before, and about the sun-rising in like manner were the Frenchmen. The same morning betimes the cardinal came again to the French host and thought by his preaching to pacify the parties; but then the Frenchmen said to him: 'Return whither ye will: bring hither no more words of treaty nor peace: and ye love

The Battle of Poitiers

yourself depart shortly.' When the cardinal saw that he travailed in vain, he took leave of the king and then he went to the prince and said: 'Sir, do what ye can: there is no remedy but to abide the battle, for I can find none accord in the French king.' Then the prince said: 'The same is our intent and all our people: God help the right!' So the cardinal returned to Poitiers. In his company there were certain knights and squires, men of arms, who were more favourable to the French king than to the prince: and when they saw that the parties should fight, they stale from their masters and went to the French host; and they made their captain the chatelain of Amposte,[§] who was as then there with the cardinal, who knew nothing thereof till he was come to Poitiers.

The certainty of the order of the Englishmen was shewed to the French king, except they had ordained three hundred men a-horseback and as many archers a-horseback to coast under covert of the mountain and to strike into the battle of the duke of Normandy, who was under the mountain afoot. This ordinance they had made of new, that the Frenchmen knew not of. The prince was with his battle down among the vines and had closed in the weakest part with their carriages.

Now will I name some of the principal lords and knights that were there with the prince: the earl of Warwick, the earl of Suffolk, the earl of Salisbury, the earl of Oxford, the lord Raynold Cobham, the lord Spencer, the lord James Audley, the lord Peter his brother, the lord Berkeley, the lord Bassett, the lord Warin, the lord Delaware, the lord Manne, the lord Willoughby, the lord Bartholomew de Burghersh, the lord of Felton, the lord Richard of Pembroke, the lord Stephen of Cosington, the lord Bradetane and other Englishmen; and of Gascon there was the lord of Pommiers, the lord of Languiran, the captal of Buch, the lord John of Caumont, the lord de Lesparre, the lord of Rauzan, the lord of Condon, the lord of

---

[§] Amposta, a fortress in Catalonia.

Montferrand, the lord of Landiras, the lord Soudic of Latrau and other that I cannot name; and of Hainowes the lord Eustace d'Aubrecicourt, the lord John of Ghistelles, and two other strangers, the lord Daniel Pasele and the lord Denis of Morbeke: all the prince's company passed not an eight thousand men one and other, and the Frenchmen were a sixty thousand fighting men, whereof there were more than three thousand knights.

Of the Battle of Poitiers between the Prince of Wales and the French King

WHEN the prince saw that he should have battle and that the cardinal was gone without any peace or truce making, and saw that the French king did set but little store by him, he said then to his men: 'Now, sirs, though we be but a small company as in regard to the puissance of our enemies, let us not be abashed therefor; for the victory lieth not in the multitude of people, but whereas God will send it. If it fortune that the journey be ours, we shall be the most honoured people of all the world; and if we die in our right quarrel, I have the king my father and brethren, and also ye have good friends and kinsmen; these shall revenge us. Therefore, sirs, for God's sake I require you do your devoirs this day; for if God be pleased and Saint George, this day ye shall see me a good knight.' These words and such other that the prince spake comforted all his people. The lord sir John Chandos that day never went from the prince, nor also the lord James Audley of a great season; but when he saw that they should needs fight, he said to the prince: 'Sir, I have served always truly my lord your father and you also, and shall do as long as I live. I say this because I made once a vow that the first battle that other the king your father or any of his children should be at, how that I would be one of the first setters on,[*] or else to die in the pain: therefore I require your grace, as in reward for any service that ever I did to the king your father or to you, that you will give me licence to depart from you and to set myself thereas I may accomplish my vow.' The prince

---

[*] 'The first setter-on and the best combatant.'

accorded to his desire and said, 'Sir James, God give you this day that grace to be the best knight of all other,' and so took him by the hand. Then the knight departed from the prince and went to the foremost front of all the battles, all only accompanied with four squires, who promised not to fail him. This lord James was a right sage and a valiant knight, and by him was much of the host ordained and governed the day before. Thus sir James was in front of the battle ready to fight with the battle of the marshals of France. In like wise the lord Eustace d'Aubrecicourt did his pain to be one of the foremost to set on. When sir James Audley began to set forward to his enemies, it fortuned to sir Eustace d'Aubrecicourt as ye shall hear after. Ye have heard before how the Almains in the French host were appointed to be still a-horseback. Sir Eustace being a-horseback laid his spear in the rest and ran into the French battle, and then a knight of Almaine, called the lord Louis of Recombes, who bare a shield silver, five roses gules, and sir Eustace bare ermines, two branches of gules,[†] -- when this Almain saw the lord Eustace come from his company, he rode against him and they met so rudely, that both knights fell to the earth. The Almain was hurt in the shoulder, therefore he rose not so quickly as did sir Eustace, who when he was up and had taken his breath, he came to the other knight as he lay on the ground; but then five other knights of Almaine came on him all at once and bare him to the earth, and so perforce there he was taken prisoner and brought to the earl of Nassau, who as then took no heed of him; and I cannot say whether they sware him prisoner or no, but they tied him to a chare and there let him stand.[‡]

Then the battle began on all parts, and the battles of the marshals of France approached, and they set forth that were appointed to break the array of the archers. They entered a-horseback into the way where the great hedges were on both

---

[†] That is, two hamedes (cut-off bars) gules on a field ermine.

[‡] 'They tied him on to a cart with their harness.'

The Battle of Poitiers

sides set full of archers. As soon as the men of arms entered, the archers began to shoot on both sides and did slay and hurt horses and knights, so that the horses when they felt the sharp arrows they would in no wise go forward, but drew aback and flang[§] and took on so fiercely, that many of them fell on their masters, so that for press they could not rise again; insomuch that the marshals' battle could never come at the prince. Certain knights and squires that were well horsed passed through the archers and thought to approach to the prince, but they could not. The lord James Audley with his four squires was in the front of that battle and there did marvels in arms, and by great prowess he came and fought with sir Arnold d'Audrehem under his own banner, and there they fought long together and sir Arnold was there sore handled. The battle of the marshals began to disorder by reason of the shot of the archers with the aid of the men of arms, who came in among them and slew of them and did what they list, and there was the lord Arnold d'Audrehem taken prisoner by other men than by sir James Audley or by his four squires; for that day he never took prisoner, but always fought and went on his enemies.

Also on the French party the lord John Clermont fought under his own banner as long as he could endure: but there he was beaten down and could not be relieved nor ransomed, but was slain without mercy: some said it was because of the words that he had the day before to sir John Chandos. So within a short space the marshals' battles were discomfited, for they fell one upon another and could not go forth;[**] and the Frenchmen that were behind and could not get forward reculed back and came on the battle of the duke of Normandy, the which was great and thick and were afoot, but anon they began to open behind;[††] for

---

[§] flang = flung?

[**] 'Ne pooient aler avant.'

[††] 'Which was great and thick in front (pardevant), but anon it became open and thin behind.'

when they knew that the marshals' battle was discomfited, they took their horses and departed, he that might best. Also they saw a rout of Englishmen coming down a little mountain a-horseback, and many archers with them, who brake in on the side of the duke's battle. True to say, the archers did their company that day great advantage; for they shot so thick that the Frenchmen wist not on what side to take heed, and little and little the Englishmen won ground on them.

And when the men of arms of England saw that the marshals' battle was discomfited and that the duke's battle began to disorder and open, they leapt then on their horses, the which they had ready by them: then they assembled together and cried, 'Saint George! Guyenne!' and the lord Chandos said to the prince: 'Sir, take your horse and ride forth; this journey is yours: God is this day in your hands: get us to the French king's battle, for their lieth all the sore of the matter. I think verily by his valiantness he will not fly: I trust we shall have him by the grace of God and Saint George, so he be well fought withal: and, sir, I heard you say that this day I should see you a good knight.' The prince said, 'Let us go forth; ye shall not see me this day return back,' and said, 'Advance, banner, in the name of God and of Saint George.' The knight that bare it did his commandment: there was then a sore battle and a perilous, and many a man overthrown, and he that was once down could not be relieved again without great succour and aid. As the prince rode and entered in among his enemies, he saw on his right hand in a little bush lying dead the lord Robert of Duras and his banner by him,‡‡ and a ten or twelve of his men about him. Then the prince said to two of his squires and to three archers: 'Sirs, take the body of this knight on a targe§§ and bear him to Poitiers, and present him from me to the cardinal of Perigord, and say how I

---

‡‡ The original adds, 'qui estoit de France au sentoir (sautoir) de gueulles.'

§§ targe = a type of shield.

The Battle of Poitiers

salute him by that token.' And this was done. The prince was informed that the cardinal's men were on the field against him, the which was not pertaining to the right order of arms, for men of the church that cometh and goeth for treaty of peace ought not by reason to bear harness nor to fight for neither of the parties; they ought to be indifferent: and because these men had done so, the prince was displeased with the cardinal, and therefore he sent unto him his nephew the lord Robert of Duras dead: and the chatelain of Amposte was taken, and the prince would have had his head stricken off because he was pertaining to the cardinal, but then the lord Chandos said: 'Sir, suffer for a season: intend to a greater matter: and peradventure the cardinal will make such excuse that ye shall be content.' Then the prince and his company dressed them on the battle of the duke of Athens, constable of France. There was many a man slain and cast to the earth. As the Frenchmen fought in companies, they cried, 'Mountjoy! Saint Denis!' and the Englishmen, 'Saint George! Guyenne!' Anon the prince with his company met with the battle of Almains, whereof the earl of Sarrebruck, the earl Nassau and the earl Nidau were captains, but in a short space they were put to flight: the archers shot so wholly together that none durst come in their dangers: they slew many a man that could not come to no ransom: these three earls was there slain, and divers other knights and squires of their company, and there was the lord d'Aubrecicourt rescued by his own men and set on horseback, and after he did that day many feats of arms and took good prisoners. When the duke of Normandy's battle saw the prince approach, they thought to save themselves, and so the duke and the king's children, the earl of Poitiers and the earl of Touraine, who were right young, believed their governours and so departed from the field, and with them more than eight hundred spears, that strake no stroke that day. Howbeit the lord Guichard d'Angle and the lord John of Saintre, who were with the earl of Poitiers, would not fly, but entered into the thickest press of the battle. The king's three sons took the way to Chauvigny, and the lord John of Landas and the lord Thibauld of Vaudenay, who were set to await on the duke of Normandy, when they had brought the duke a long league from the battle, then they took leave of the duke and desired the lord of Saint-Venant that he should not leave the duke, but to bring him in safeguard, whereby he should win more thank of the king than to abide still in the field. Then they met also the duke of Orleans and a great company with him, who were also departed from the field with clear hands: there were many good knights and squires, though that their masters departed from the field, yet they had rather a died than to have had any reproach.

   Then the king's battle came on the Englishmen: there was a sore fight and many a great stroke given and received. The king and his youngest son met with the battle of the English marshals, the earl of Warwick and the earl of Suffolk, and with them of Gascons the captal of Buch, the lord of Pommiers, the lord Amery of Tastes, the lord of Mussidan, the lord of Languiran and the lord de Latrau. To the French party there came time enough the lord John of Landas and the lord of Vaudenay; they alighted afoot and went into the king's battle, and a little beside fought the duke of Athens, constable of France, and a little above him the duke of Bourbon and many good knights of Bourbonnais and of Picardy with him, and a little on the one side there were the Poitevins, the lord de Pons, the lord of Partenay, the lord of Dammartin, the lord of Tannay-Bouton, the lord of Surgieres, the lord John Saintre, the lord Guichard d'Angle, the lord Argenton, the lord of Linieres, the lord of Montendre and divers other, also the viscount of Rochechouart and the earl of Aunay;[***] and of Burgoyne the lord James of Beaujeu, the lord de Chateau-Vilain and other: in another part there was the earl of Ventadour and of Montpensier, the lord James of Bourbon, the lord John d'Artois and also the lord James his brother, the lord Arnold of Cervolles, called the archpriest, armed for the young earl of Alencon ; and of Auvergne there was the lord of Mercoeur, the lord de la Tour, the lord of Alencon, the lord of Montaigu, the lord of Rochfort,

---

[***] 'Le conte d'Aulnoy,' but it should be 'visconte.'

The Battle of Poitiers

the lord d'Acier, the lord d'Acon; and of Limousin there was the lord de Melval, the lord of Mareuil, the lord of Pierrebuffiere; and of Picardy there was the lord William of Nesle, the lord Arnold of Rayneval, the lord Geoffrey of Saint-Dizier, the lord of Chauny, the lord of Helly, the lord of Montsault, the lord of Hangest and divers other: and also in the king's battle there was the earl Douglas of Scotland, who fought a season right valiantly, but when he saw the discomfiture, he departed and saved himself; for in no wise he would be taken of the Englishmen, he had rather been there slain. On the English part the lord James Audley with the aid of his four squires fought always in the chief of the battle: he was sore hurt in the body and in the visage: as long as his breath served him he fought; at last at the end of the battle his four squires took and brought him out of the field and laid him under a hedge side for to refresh him; and they unarmed him and bound up his wounds as well as they could. On the French party king John was that day a full right good knight: if the fourth part of his men had done their devoirs as well as he did, the journey had been his by all likelihood. Howbeit they were all slain and taken that were there, except a few that saved themselves, that were with the king.[†††] There was slain the duke Peter of Bourbon, the lord Guichard of Beaujeu, the lord of Landas, and the duke of Athens, constable of France, the bishop of Chalons in Champagne, the lord William of Nesle, the lord Eustace of Ribemont, the lord de la Tour, the lord William of Montaigu, sir Grismouton of Chambly, sir Baudrin de la Heuse, and many other, as they fought by companies; and there were taken prisoners the lord of Vaudenay, the lord of Pompadour, and the archpriest, sore hurt, the earl of Vaudimont, the earl of Mons, the earl of Joinville, the earl of Vendome, sir Louis of Melval, the lord Pierrebuffiere and the lord of Serignac:

[†††] 'Howbeit they that stayed acquitted them as well as they might, so that they were all slain or taken. Few escaped of those that set themselves with the king': or according to the fuller text: 'Few escaped of those that alighted down on the sand by the side of the king their lord.'

there were at that brunt, slain and taken more than two hundred knights.‡‡‡

---

‡‡‡ The translator has chosen to rearrange the above list of killed, wounded or taken, which the French text gives in order as they fought, saying that in one part there fell the duke of Bourbon, sir Guichard of Beaujeu and sir John of Landas, and there were severely wounded or taken: the archpriest, sir Thibaud of Vodenay and sir Baudouin d'Annequin; in another there were slain the duke of Athens and the bishop of Chalons, and taken the earl of Vaudemont and Joinville and the earl of Vendome: a little above this there were slain sir William de Nesle, sir Eustace de Ribemont and others, and taken sir Louis de Melval, the lord of Pierrebuffiere and the lord of Seregnach.

Of two Frenchmen that fled from the Battle of Poitiers and two Englishmen that followed them

AMONG the battles, recounterings, chases and pursuits that were made that day in the field, it fortuned so to sir Oudart of Renty that when he departed from the field because he saw the field was lost without recovery, he thought not to abide the danger of the Englishmen; wherefore he fled all alone and was gone out of the field a league, and an English knight pursued him and ever cried to him and said, 'Return again, sir knight, it is a shame to fly away thus.'

Then the knight turned, and the English knight thought to have stricken him with his spear in the targe, but he failed, for sir Oudart swerved aside from the stroke, but he failed not the English knight, for he strake him such a stroke on the helm with his sword, that he was astonied[*] and fell from his horse to the earth and lay still. Then sir Oudart alighted and came to him or he could rise, and said, 'Yield you, rescue or no rescue, or else I shall slay you.' The Englishman yielded and went with him, and afterward was ransomed. Also it fortuned that another squire of Picardy called John de Hellenes was fled from the battle and met with his page, who delivered him a new fresh horse, whereon he rode away alone. The same season there was in the field the lord Berkeley of England, a young lusty knight, who the same day reared his banner, and he all alone pursued the said John of

---

[*] astonied = stunned.

Hellenes. And when he had followed the space of a league, the said John turned again and laid his sword in the rest instead of a spear, and so came running toward the lord Berkeley, who lift up his sword to have stricken the squire; but when he saw the stroke come, he turned from it, so that the Englishman lost his stroke and John strake him as he passed on the arm, that the lord Berkeley's sword fell into the field. When he saw his sword down, he lighted suddenly off his horse and came to the place where his sword lay, and as he stooped down to take up his sword, the French squire did pike his sword at him, and by hap strake him through both the thighs, so that the knight fell to the earth and could not help himself. And John alighted off his horse and took the knight's sword that lay on the ground, and came to him and demanded if he would yield him or not. The knight then demanded his name. 'Sir,' said he, 'I hight[†] John of Hellenes; but what is your name?' 'Certainly,' said the knight, 'my name is Thomas and am lord of Berkeley, a fair castle on the river of Severn in the marches of Wales.' 'Well, sir,' quoth the squire, 'then ye shall be my prisoner, and I shall bring you in safe-guard and I shall see that you shall be healed of your hurt.' 'Well,' said the knight, 'I am content to be your prisoner, for ye have by law of arms won me.' There he sware to be his prisoner, rescue or no rescue. Then the squire drew forth the sword out of the knight's thighs and the wound was open: then he wrapped and bound the wound and set him on his horse and so brought him fair and easily to Chatelleraut, and there tarried more than fifteen days for his sake and did get him remedy for his hurt: and when he was somewhat amended, then he gat him a litter and so brought him at his ease to his house in Picardy. There he was more than a year till he was perfectly whole; and when he departed he paid for his ransom six thousand nobles, and so this squire was made a knight by reason of the profit that he had of the lord Berkeley.

[†] hight = be called.

How King John was taken prisoner at the Battle of Poitiers

OFTENTIMES the adventures of amours and of war are more fortunate and marvellous than any man can think or wish. Truly this battle, the which was near to Poitiers in the fields of Beauvoir and Maupertuis, was right great and perilous, and many deeds of arms there was done the which all came not to knowledge. The fighters on both sides endured much pain: king John with his own hands did that day marvels in arms: he had an axe in his hands wherewith he defended himself and fought in the breaking of the press. Near to the king there was taken the earl of Tancarville, sir Jaques of Bourbon earl of Ponthieu, and the lord John of Artois earl of Eu, and a little above that under the banner of the captal of Buch was taken sir Charles of Artois and divers other knights and squires. The chase endured to the gates of Poitiers: there were many slain and beaten down, horse and man, for they of Poitiers closed their gates and would suffer none to enter; wherefore in the street before the gate was horrible murder, men hurt and beaten down. The Frenchmen yielded themselves as far off as they might know an Englishman: there were divers English archers that had four, five or six prisoners: the lord of Pons, a great baron of Poitou, was there slain, and many other knights and squires; and there was taken the earl of Rochechouart, the lord of Dammartin, the lord of Partenay, and of Saintonge the lord of Montendre and the lord John of Saintre, but he was so sore hurt that he had never health after: he was reputed for one of the best knights in France. And there was left for dead among other dead men the lord Guichard d'Angle, who fought that day by the king right valiantly, and so did the lord of Chamy, on whom was great press, because he bare the sovereign banner of the king's: his own banner was also in the field, the which was of gules[*], three scutcheons[†] silver. So many Englishmen and Gascons come to that part, that perforce they opened the king's battle, so that the Frenchmen were so mingled among their enemies that sometime there was five men upon one gentleman. There was taken the lord of Pompadour and[‡] the lord Bartholomew de Burghersh, and there was slain sir Geoffrey of Charny with the king's banner in his hands: also the lord Raynold Cobham slew the earl of Dammartin. Then there was a great press to take the king, and such as knew him cried, 'Sir, yield you, or else ye are but dead.' There was a knight of Saint-Omer's, retained in wages with the king of England, called sir Denis Morbeke, who had served the Englishmen five year before, because in his youth he had forfeited the realm of France for a murder that he did at Saint-Omer's. It happened so well for him, that he was next to the king when they were about to take him: he stept forth into the press, and by strength of his body and arms he came to the French king and said in good French, 'Sir, yield you.' The king beheld the knight and said: 'To whom shall I yield me? Where is my cousin the prince of Wales? If I might see him, I would speak with him.' Denis answered and said: 'Sir, he is not here; but yield you to me and I shall bring you to him. 'Who be you?' quoth the king. 'Sir,' quoth he, 'I am Denis of Morbeke, a knight of Artois; but I serve the king of England because I am banished the realm of France and I have forfeited all that I had there.' Then the king gave him his right gauntlet, saying, 'I yield me to you.' There was a great press about the king, for every man enforced him to say,[§] 'I have taken him,' so

---

[*] gules = red (in heraldry).

[†] scutcheon = shield.

[‡] This 'and' should be 'by,' but the French text is responsible for the mistake.

[§] 'S'efforcoit de dire.'

The Battle of Poitiers

that the king could not go forward with his young son the lord Philip with him because of the press.

The prince of Wales, who was courageous and cruel as a lion, took that day great pleasure to fight and to chase his enemies. The lord John Chandos, who was with him, of all that day never left him nor never took heed of taking of any prisoner: then at the end of the battle he said to the prince: 'Sir, it were good that you rested here and set your banner a-high in this bush, that your people may draw hither, for they be sore spread abroad, nor I can see no more banners nor pennons of the French party; wherefore, sir, rest and refresh you, for ye be sore chafed.' Then the prince's banner was set up a-high on a bush, and trumpets and clarions began to sown. Then the prince did off his bassenet[**], and the knights for his body and they of his chamber were ready about him, and a red pavilion pight up, and then drink was brought forth to the prince and for such lords as were about him, the which still increased as they came from the chase: there they tarried and their prisoners with them. And when the two marshals were come to the prince, he demanded of them if they knew any tiding of the French king. They answered and said: 'Sir, we hear none of certainty, but we think verily he is other dead or taken, for he is not gone out of the battles.' Then the prince said to the earl of Warwick and to sir Raynold Cobham: 'Sirs, I require you go forth and see what ye can know, that at your return ye may shew me the truth.' These two lords took their horses and departed from the prince and rode up a little hill to look about them: then they perceived a flock of men of arms coming together right wearily:[††] there was the French king afoot in great peril, for Englishmen and Gascons were his masters; they had taken him from sir Denis Morbeke perforce, and such as were most of force said, 'I have taken him.' 'Nay,' quoth another, 'I have taken him': so they strave which should

---

[**] bassenet = a type of helmet, now usually spelt bascinet.
[††] 'Lentement.'

have him. Then the French king, to eschew that peril, said: 'Sirs, strive not: lead me courteously, and my son, to my cousin the prince, and strive not for my taking, for I am so great a lord to make you all rich.' The king's words somewhat appeased them; howbeit ever as they went they made riot and brawled for the taking of the king. When the two foresaid lords saw and heard that noise and strife among them, they came to them and said: 'Sirs, what is the matter that ye strive for?' 'Sirs,' said one of them, 'it is for the French king, who is here taken prisoner, and there be more than ten knights and squires that challengeth the taking of him and of his son.' Then the two lords entered into the press and caused every man to draw aback, and commanded them in the prince's name on pain of their heads to make no more noise nor to approach the king no nearer, without they were commanded. Then every man gave room to the lords, and they alighted and did their reverence to the king, and so brought him and his son in peace and rest to the prince of Wales.

Of the gift that the Prince gave to the Lord Audley after the Battle of Poitiers

As soon as the earl of Warwick and the lord Cobham were departed from the prince, as ye have heard before, then the prince demanded of the knights that were about him for the lord Audley, if any knew anything of him. Some knights that were there answered and said: 'Sir, he is sore hurt and lieth in a litter here beside.' 'By my faith,' said the prince, 'of his hurts I am right sorry: go and know if he may be brought hither, or else I will go and see him thereas he is.' Then two knights came to the lord Audley and said: 'Sir, the prince desireth greatly to see you, other ye must go to him or else he will come to you.' 'Ah, sir,' said the knight, 'I thank the prince when he thinketh on so poor a knight as I am.' Then he called eight of his servants and caused them to bear him in his litter to the place whereas the prince was. Then the prince took him in his arms and kissed him and made him great cheer and said: 'Sir James, I ought greatly to honour you, for by your valiance ye have this day achieved the grace and renown of us all, and ye are reputed for the most valiant of all other.' 'Ah, sir,' said the knight, 'ye say as it pleaseth you: I would it were so: and if I have this day anything advanced myself to serve you and to accomplish the vow that I made, it ought not to be reputed to me any prowess.' 'Sir James,' said the prince, 'I and all ours take you in this journey for the best doer in arms, and to the intent to furnish you the better to pursue the wars, I retain you for ever to be my knight with five hundred marks of yearly revenues, the which I shall assign you on mine heritage in England.' 'Sir,' said the knight, 'God grant me to deserve the great goodness that ye shew me': and so he took his leave of the prince, for he was right feeble, and so his servants brought him to his lodging. And as soon as he was gone, the earl of Warwick and the lord Cobham returned to the prince and presented to him the French king. The prince made lowly reverence to the king and caused wine and spices to be brought forth, and himself served the king in sign of great love.

How the Englishmen won greatly at the Battle of Poitiers

THUS, this battle was discomfited, as ye have heard, the which was in the fields of Maupertuis a two leagues from Poitiers the twenty-second day of September the year of our Lord MCCCLVI. It begun in the morning[*] and ended at noon, but as then all the Englishmen were not returned from the chase; therefore the prince's banner stood on a bush to draw all his men together, but it was well nigh night or all came from the chase. And as it was reported, there was slain all the flower of France, and there was taken with the king and the lord Philip his son a seventeen earls, beside barons, knights and squires, and slain a five or six thousand of one and other. When every man was come from the chase, they had twice as many prisoners as they were in number in all. Then it was counselled among them because of the great charge and doubt to keep so many, that they should put many of them to ransom incontinent in the field, and so they did: and the prisoners found the Englishmen and Gascons right courteous; there were many that day put to ransom and let go all only on their promise of faith and truth to return again between that and Christmas to Bordeaux with their ransoms. Then that night they lay in the field beside whereas the battle had been: some unarmed them, but not all, and unarmed all their prisoners, and every man made good cheer to his prisoner; for that day whosoever took any prisoner, he was clear his and might quit or ransom him at his pleasure. All such as were there with the prince were all made rich with honour and

---

[*] 'Environ heure de prime.'

goods, as well by ransoming of prisoners as by winning of gold, silver, plate, jewels, that was there found: there was no man that did set anything by rich harness, whereof there was great plenty, for the Frenchmen came thither richly beseen, weening to have had the journey for them.

How the Lord James Audley gave to his four squires the five hundred marks of revenues that the Prince had given him

WHEN sir James Audley was brought to his lodging, then he sent for sir Peter Audley his brother and for the lord Bartholomew of Burghersh, the lord Stephen of Cosington, the lord of Willoughby and the lord Ralph Ferrers, all these were of his lineage, and then he called before him his four squires, that had served him that day well and truly. Then he said to the said lords: 'Sirs, it hath pleased my lord the prince to give me five hundred marks of revenues by year in heritage, for the which gift I have done him but small service with my body. Sirs, behold here these four squires, who hath always served me truly and specially this day: that honour that I have is by their valiantness. Wherefore I will reward them: I give and resign into their hands the gift that my lord the prince hath given me of five hundred marks of yearly revenues, to them and to their heirs for ever, in like manner as it was given me. I clearly disherit me thereof and inherit them without any repeal[*] or condition.' The lords and other that ere there, every man beheld other and said among themselves: 'It cometh of a great nobleness to give this gift.' They answered him with one voice: 'Sir, be it as God will; we shall bear witness in this behalf wheresoever we be come.' Then they departed from him, and some of them went to the prince, who the same night would make a supper to the French king and

---

[*] 'Rappel,' i. e. power of recalling the gift. The word 'repeal' is a correction of 'rebell.'

The Chronicles of Froissart

to the prisoners, for they had enough to do withal, of that the Frenchmen brought with them,† for the Englishmen wanted victual before, for some in three days had no bread before.

---

† 'Who was to give the king of France a supper of his own provisions: for the French had brought great abundance with them, and provisions had failed among the English,' etc.

How the Prince made a supper to the French King the same day of the battle

THE same day of the battle at night the prince made a supper in his lodging to the French king and to the most part of the great lords that were prisoners. The prince made the king and his son, the lord James of Bourbon, the lord John d'Artois, the earl of Tancarville, the earl of Estampes, the earl Dammartin, the earl of Joinville and the lord of Partenay to sit all at one board, and other lords, knights and squires at other tables; and always the prince served before the king as humbly as he could, and would not sit at the king's board for any desire that the king could make, but he said he was not sufficient to sit at the table with so great a prince as the king was. But then he said to the king: 'Sir, for God's sake make none evil nor heavy cheer, though God this day did not consent to follow your will; for, sir, surely the king my father shall bear you as much honour and amity as he may do, and shall accord with you so reasonably that ye shall ever be friends together after. And, sir, methinks ye ought to rejoice, though the journey be not as ye would have had it, for this day ye have won the high renown of prowess and have passed this day in valiantness all other of your party. Sir, I say not this to mock you, for all that be on our party, that saw every man's deeds, are plainly accorded by true sentence to give you the prize and chaplet.' Therewith the Frenchmen began to murmur and said among themselves how the prince had spoken nobly, and that by all estimation he should prove a noble man, if God send him life and to persevere in such good fortune.

How the Prince returned to Bordeaux after the Battle of Poitiers

WHEN supper was done, every man went to his lodging with their prisoners. The same night they put many to ransom and believed them on their faiths and troths, and ransomed them but easily, for they said they would set no knight's ransom so high, but that he might pay at his ease and maintain still his degree. The next day, when they had heard mass and taken some repast and that everything was trussed and ready, then they took their horses and rode towards Poitiers. The same night there was come to Poitiers the lord of Roye with a hundred spears: he was not at the battle, but he met the duke of Normandy near to Chauvigny, and the duke sent him to Poitiers to keep the town till they heard other tidings. When the lord of Roye knew that the Englishmen were so near coming to the city, he caused every man to be armed and every man to go to his defence to the walls, towers and gates; and the Englishmen passed by without any approaching, for they were so laded with gold, silver and prisoners, that in their returning they assaulted no fortress; they thought it a great deed if they might bring the French king, with their other prisoners and riches that they had won, in safeguard to Bordeaux. They rode but small journeys because of their prisoners and great carriages that they had: they rode in a day no more but four or five leagues and lodged ever betimes, and rode close together in good array saving the marshals' battles, who rode ever before with five hundred men of arms to open the passages as the prince should pass; but they found no encounters, for all the country was so frayed that every man drew to the fortresses.

The Battle of Poitiers

As the prince rode, it was shewed him how the lord Audley had given to his four squires the gift of the five hundred marks that he had given unto him: then the prince sent for him and he was brought in his litter to the prince, who received him courteously and said: 'Sir James, we have knowledge that the revenues that we gave you, as soon as ye came to your lodging, you gave the same to four squires: we would know why ye did so, and whether the gift was agreeable to you or not.' 'Sir,' said the knight, 'it is of truth I have given it to them, and I shall shew you why I did so. These four squires that be here present have a long season served me well and truly in many great businesses and, sir, in this last battle they served me in such wise that an they had never done nothing else I was bound to reward them, and before the same day they had never nothing of me in reward. Sir, I am but a man alone; but by the aid and comfort of them I took on me to accomplish my vow long before made. I had been dead in the battle an they had not been: wherefore, sir, when I considered the love that they bare unto me, I had not been courteous if I would not a rewarded them. I thank God I have had and shall have enough as long as I live: I will never be abashed for lack of good. Sir, if I have done this without your pleasure, I require you to pardon me, for, sir, both I and my squires shall serve you as well as ever we did.' Then the prince said: 'Sir James, for anything that ye have done I cannot blame you, but can you good thank therefor; and for the valiantness of these squires, whom ye praise so much, I accord to them your gift, and I will render again to you six hundred marks in like manner as ye had the other.'

Thus the prince and his company did so much that they passed through Poitou and Saintonge without damage and came to Blaye, and there passed the river of Gironde and arrived in the good city of Bordeaux. It cannot be recorded the great feast and cheer that they of the city with the clergy made to the prince, and how honourably they were there received. The prince brought the French king into the abbey of Saint Andrew's, and there they lodged both, the king in one part and the prince in the other. The prince bought of the lords, knights and squires of Gascoyne the most part of the earls of the realm of France, such as were prisoners, and paid ready money for them. There was divers questions and challenges made between the knights and squires of Gascoyne for taking of the French king; howbeit Denis Morbeke by right of arms and by true tokens that he shewed challenged him for his prisoner. Another squire of Gascoyne called Bernard of Truttes said how he had right to him: there was much ado and many words before the prince and other lords that were there, and because these two challenged each other to fight in that quarrel, the prince caused the matter to rest till they came in England and that no declaration should be made but afore the king of England his father; but because the French king himself aided to sustain the challenge of Denis Morbeke, for he inclined more to him than to any other, the prince therefore privily caused to be delivered to the said sir Denis two thousand nobles to maintain withal his estate.

Anon after the prince came to Bordeaux, the cardinal of Perigord came thither, who was sent from the pope in legation, as it was said. He was there more than fifteen days or the prince would speak with him because of the chatelain of Amposte and his men, who were against him in the battle of Poitiers. The prince believed that the cardinal sent them thither, but the cardinal did so much by the means of the lord of Caumont, the lord of Montferrand and the captal of Buch, who were his cousins, they shewed so good reasons to the prince, that he was content to hear him speak. And when he was before the prince, he excused himself so sagely that the prince and his council held him excused, and so he fell again into the prince's love and redeemed out his men by reasonable ransoms; and the chatelain was set to his ransom of ten thousand franks, the which he paid after. Then the cardinal began to treat on the deliverance of the French king, but I pass it briefly because nothing was done. Thus the prince, the Gascons and Englishmen tarried still at Bordeaux till it was Lent in great mirth and revel, and spent foolishly the gold and silver that they had won. In England also there was

The Battle of Poitiers

great joy when they heard tidings of the battle of Poitiers, of the discomfiting of the Frenchmen and taking of the king: great solemnities were made in all churches and great fires and wakes throughout all England. The knights and squires, such as were come home from that journey, were much made of and praised more than other.

Chapter 3
Wat Tyler's Rebellion

How the Commons of England rebelled against the Noblemen

IN the mean season while this treaty was, there fell in England great mischief and rebellion of moving of the common people, by which deed England was at a point to have been lost without recovery. There was never realm nor country in so great adventure as it was in that time, and all because of the ease and riches that the common people were of, which moved them to this rebellion, as sometime they did in France, the which did much hurt, for by such incidents the realm of France hath been greatly grieved.

It was a marvellous thing and of poor foundation that this mischief began in England, and to give ensample to all manner of people I will speak thereof as it was done, as I was informed, and of the incidents thereof. There was an usage in England, and yet is in divers countries, that the noblemen hath great franchise over the commons and keepeth them in servage, that is to say, their tenants ought by custom to labour the lords' lands, to gather and bring home their corns, and some to thresh and to fan, and by servage to make their hay and to hew their wood and bring it home. All these things they ought to do by servage, and there be more of these people in England than in any other realm. Thus the noblemen and prelates are served by them, and especially in the county of Kent, Essex, Sussex and Bedford. These unhappy people of these said countries began to stir, because they said they were kept in great servage, and in the beginning of the world, they said, there were no bondmen, wherefore they maintained that none ought to be bond, without he did treason to his lord, as Lucifer did to God; but they said they could have no such battle,* for they were neither angels nor spirits, but men formed to the similitude of their lords, saying why should they then be kept so under like beasts; the which they said they would no longer suffer, for they would be all one, and if they laboured or did anything for their lords, they would have wages therefor as well as other. And of this imagination was a foolish priest in the country of Kent called John Ball, for the which foolish words he had been three times in the bishop of Canterbury's prison: for this priest used oftentimes on the Sundays after mass, when the people were going out of the minster, to go into the cloister and preach, and made the people to assemble about him, and would say thus: 'Ah, ye good people, the matters goeth not well to pass in England, nor shall not do till everything be common, and that there be no villains nor gentlemen, but that we may be all unied together, and that the lords be no greater masters than we be. What have we deserved, or why should we be kept thus in servage? We be all come from one father and one mother, Adam and Eve: whereby can they say or shew that they be greater lords than we be, saving by that they cause us to win and labour for that they dispend? They are clothed in velvet and camlet furred with grise†, and we be vestured with poor cloth: they have their wines, spices and good bread, and we have the drawing out of the chaff‡ and drink water: they dwell in fair houses, and we have the pain and travail, rain and wind in the fields; and by that that cometh of our labours they keep and maintain their estates: we be called their bondmen, and without we do readily them

---

* The true text is, 'Mais ils n'avoient pas cette taille,' 'but they were not of that nature.' The translator found the corruption 'bataille' for 'taille.'

† grise = rabbit?

‡ Froissart says 'le seigle, le retrait et la paille,' 'the rye, the bran and the straw.' The translator's French text had 'le seigle, le retraict de la paille.'

service, we be beaten; and we have no sovereign to whom we may complain, nor that will hear us nor do us right. Let us go to the king, he is young, and shew him what servage we be in, and shew him how we will have it otherwise, or else we will provide us of some remedy; and if we go together, all manner of people that be now in any bondage will follow us to the intent to be made free; and when the king seeth us, we shall have some remedy, either by fairness or otherwise.' Thus John Ball said on Sundays, when the people issued out of the churches in the villages; wherefore many of the mean people loved him, and such as intended to no goodness said how he said truth; and so they would murmur one with another in the fields and in the ways as they went together, affirming how John Ball said truth.

The archbishop of Canterbury, who was informed of the saying of this John Ball, caused him to be taken and put in prison a two or three months to chastise him: howbeit, it had been much better at the beginning that he had been condemned to perpetual prison or else to have died, rather than to have suffered him to have been again delivered out of prison; but the bishop had conscience to let him die. And when this John Ball was out of prison, he returned again to his error, as he did before.

Of his words and deeds there were much people in London informed, such as had great envy at them that were rich and such as were noble; and then they began to speak among them and said how the realm of England was right evil governed, and how that gold and silver was taken from them by them that were named noblemen: so thus these unhappy men of London began to rebel and assembled them together, and sent word to the foresaid countries that they should come to London and bring their people with them, promising them how they should find London open to receive them and the commons of the city to be of the same accord, saying how they would do so much to the king that there should not be one bondman in all England.

This promise moved so them of Kent, of Essex, of Sussex, of Bedford and of the countries about, that they rose and came towards London to the number of sixty thousand. And they had a captain called Water Tyler, and with him in company was Jack Straw and John Ball: these three were chief sovereign captains, but the head of all was Water Tyler, and he was indeed a tiler of houses, an ungracious patron. When these unhappy men began thus to stir, they of London, except such as were of their band, were greatly affrayed. Then the mayor of London and the rich men of the city took counsel together, and when they saw the people thus coming on every side, they caused the gates of the city to be closed and would suffer no man to enter into the city. But when they had well imagined, they advised not so to do, for they thought they should thereby put their suburbs in great peril to be brent; and so they opened again the city, and there entered in at the gates in some place a hundred, two hundred, by twenty and by thirty, and so when they came to London, they entered and lodged: and yet of truth the third part[§] of these people could not tell what to ask or demand, but followed each other like beasts, as the shepherds[**] did of old time, saying how they would go conquer the Holy Land, and at last all came to nothing. In like wise these villains and poor people came to London, a hundred mile off, sixty mile, fifty mile, forty mile, and twenty mile off, and from all countries about London, but the most part came from the countries before named, and as they came they demanded ever for the king. The gentlemen of the countries, knights and squires, began to doubt, when they saw the people began to rebel; and though they were in doubt, it was good reason; for a less occasion they might have been affrayed. So the gentlemen drew together as well as they might.

[§] 'Bien les trois pars,' i. e. 'three-fourths.'

[**] 'Les pastoureaulx.' The reference no doubt is to the Pastoureaux of 1320, who were destroyed at Aigues-Mortes when attempting to obtain a passage to the Holy Land.

The same day that these unhappy people of Kent were coming to London, there returned from Canterbury the king's mother, princess of Wales, coming from her pilgrimage. She was in great jeopardy to have been lost, for these people came to her chare and dealt rudely with her, whereof the good lady was in great doubt lest they would have done some villainy to her or to her damosels. Howbeit, God kept her, and she came in one day from Canterbury to London, for she never durst tarry by the way. The same time king Richard her son was at the Tower of London: there his mother found him, and with him there was the earl of Salisbury, the archbishop of Canterbury, sir Robert of Namur, the lord of Gommegnies and divers other, who were in doubt of these people that thus gathered together, and wist not what they demanded. This rebellion was well known in the king's court, or any of these people began to stir out of their houses; but the king nor his council did provide no remedy therefor, which was great marvel. And to the intent that all lords and good people and such as would nothing but good should take ensample to correct them that be evil and rebellious, I shall shew you plainly all the matter, as it was.

The evil deeds that these Commons of England did to the King's Officers, and how they sent a knight to speak with the King

THE Monday before the feast of Corpus Christi the year of our Lord God a thousand three hundred and eighty-one these people issued out of their houses to come to London to speak with the king to be made free, for they would have had no bondman in England. And so first they came to Saint Thomas of Canterbury, and there John Ball had thought to have found the bishop of Canterbury, but he was at London with the king. When Wat Tyler and Jack Straw entered into Canterbury, all the common people made great feast, for all the town was of their assent; and there they took counsel to go to London to the king, and to send some of their company over the river of Thames into Essex, into Sussex and into the counties of Stafford and Bedford, to speak to the people that they should all come to the farther side of London and thereby to close London round about, so that the king should not stop their passages, and that they should all meet together on Corpus Christi day. They that were at Canterbury entered into Saint Thomas' church and did there much hurt, and robbed and brake up the bishop's chamber, and in robbing and bearing out their pillage they said: 'Ah, this chancellor of England hath had a good market to get together all this riches: he shall give us now account of the revenues of England and of the great profits that he hath gathered sith the king's coronation.' When they had this Monday thus broken the abbey of Saint Vincent, they departed in the morning and all the people of Canterbury with them, and so took the way to Rochester and sent their people to the villages about. And in

Wat Tyler's Rebellion

their going they beat down and robbed houses of advocates and procurers of the king's court and of the archbishop, and had mercy of none. And when they were come to Rochester, they had there good cheer; for the people of that town tarried for them, for they were of the same sect, and then they went to the castle there and took the knight that had the rule thereof, he was called sir John Newton, and they said to him: 'Sir, it behoveth you to go with us and you shall be our sovereign captain and to do that we will have you.' The knight excused himself honestly and shewed them divers considerations and excuses, but all availed him nothing, for they said unto him: 'Sir John, if ye do not as we will have you, ye are but dead.' The knight, seeing these people in that fury and ready to slay him, he then doubted death and agreed to them, and so they took him with them against his inward will; and in like wise did they of other counties in England, as Essex, Sussex, Stafford, Bedford and Warwick, even to Lincoln; for they brought the knights and gentlemen into such obeisance, that they caused them to go with them, whether they would or not, as the lord Moylays, a great baron, sir Stephen of Hales and sir Thomas of Cosington and other.

Now behold the great fortune. If they might have come to their intents, they would have destroyed all the noblemen of England, and thereafter all other nations would have followed the same and have taken foot and ensample by them and by them of Gaunt and Flanders, who rebelled against their lord. The same year the Parisians rebelled in like wise and found out the mallets of iron, of whom there were more than twenty thousand, as ye shall hear after in this history; but first we will speak of them of England.

When these people thus lodged at Rochester departed, and passed the river and came to Brentford, alway keeping still their opinions, beating down before them and all about the places and houses of advocates and procurers, and striking off the heads of divers persons. And so long they went forward till they came within a four mile of London, and there lodged on a hill called Blackheath; and as they went, they said ever they were the king's men and the noble commons of England:[*] and when they of London knew that they were come so near to them, the mayor, as ye have heard before, closed the gates and kept straitly all the passages. This order caused the mayor, who was called Nicholas Walworth,[†] and divers other rich burgesses of the city, who were not of their sect; but there were in London of their unhappy opinions more than thirty thousand.

Then these people thus being lodged on Blackheath determined to send their knight to speak with the king and to shew him how all that they have done or will do is for him and his honour, and how the realm of England hath not been well governed a great space for the honour of the realm nor for the common profit by his uncles and by the clergy, and specially by the archbishop of Canterbury his chancellor; whereof they would have account. This knight durst do none otherwise, but so came by the river of Thames to the Tower. The king and they that were with him in the Tower, desiring to hear tidings, seeing this knight coming made him way, and was brought before the king into a chamber; and with the king was the princess his mother and his two brethren, the earl of Kent and the lord John Holland, the earl of Salisbury, the earl of Warwick, the earl of Oxford, the archbishop of Canterbury, the lord of Saint John's,[‡] sir Robert of Namur, the lord of Vertaing, the lord of Gommegnies, sir Henry of Senzeille, the mayor of London and divers other notable burgesses. This knight sir John Newton, who was well known among them, for he was one of the king's officers, he kneeled down before the king and said: 'My right redoubted lord, let it not displease your grace the message that I must needs shew

---

[*] 'That were for the king and the noble commons (or commonwealth) of England.'

[†] Froissart calls him John: his name was really William.

[‡] That is, the grand prior of the Hospital.

you, for, dear sir, it is by force and against my will.' 'Sir John,' said the king, 'say what ye will: I hold you excused.' 'Sir, the commons of this your realm hath sent me to you to desire you to come and speak with them on Blackheath; for they desire to have none but you: and, sir, ye need not to have any doubt of your person, for they will do you no hurt; for they hold and will hold you for their king. But, sir, they say they will shew you divers things, the which shall be right necessary for you to take heed of, when they speak with you; of the which things, sir, I have no charge to shew you: but, sir, it may please you to give me an answer such as may appease them and that they may know for truth that I have spoken with you; for they have my children in hostage till I return again to them, and without I return again, they will slay my children incontinent.'

Then the king made him an answer and said: 'Sir, ye shall have an answer shortly.' Then the king took counsel what was best for him to do, and it was anon determined that the next morning the king should go down the river by water and without fail to speak with them. And when sir John Newton heard that answer, he desired nothing else and so took his leave of the king and of the lords and returned again into his vessel, and passed the Thames and went to Blackheath, where he had left more than threescore thousand men. And there he answered them that the next morning they should send some of their council to the Thames, and there the king would come and speak with them. This answer greatly pleased them, and so passed that night as well as they might, and the fourth part of them[§] fasted for lack of victual for they had none, wherewith they were sore displeased, which was good reason.

All this season the earl of Buckingham was in Wales, for there he had fair heritages by reason of his wife, who was daughter to the earl of Northumberland and Hereford; but the voice was all through London how he was among these people.

[§] 'Les quatre pars d'eux,' 'four-fifths of them.'

And some said certainly how they had seen him there among them; and all was because there was one Thomas in their company, a man of the county of Cambridge, that was very like the earl. Also the lords that lay at Plymouth to go into Portugal were well informed of this rebellion and of the people that thus began to rise; wherefore they doubted lest their viage should have been broken, or else they feared lest the commons about Hampton, Winchester and Arundel would have come on them: wherefore they weighed up their anchors and issued out of the haven with great pain, for the wind was sore against them, and so took the sea and there cast anchor abiding for the wind. And the duke of Lancaster, who was in the marches of Scotland between Moorlane and Roxburgh entreating with the Scots, where it was shewed him of the rebellion, whereof he was in doubt, for he knew well he was but little beloved with the commons of England; howbeit, for all those tidings, yet he did sagely demean himself as touching the treaty with the Scots. The earl Douglas, the earl of Moray, the earl of Sutherland and the earl Thomas Versy, and the Scots that were there for the treaty knew right well the rebellion in England, how the common people in every part began to rebel against the noblemen; wherefore the Scots thought that England was in great danger to be lost, and therefore in their treaties they were the more stiffer against the duke of Lancaster and his council.

Now let us speak of the commons of England and how they persevered.

How the Commons of England entered into London, and of the great evil that they did, and of the death of the Bishop of Canterbury and divers others

IN the morning on Corpus Christi day king Richard heard mass in the Tower of London, and all his lords, and then he took his barge with the earl of Salisbury, the earl of Warwick, the earl of Oxford and certain knights, and so rowed down along the Thames to Rotherhithe, whereas was descended down the hill a ten thousand men to see the king and to speak with him. And when they saw the king's barge coming, they began to shout, and made such a cry, as though all the devils of hell had been among them. And they had brought with them sir John Newton to the intent that, if the king had not come, they would have stricken him all to pieces, and so they had promised him. And when the king and his lords saw the demeanour of the people, the best assured of them were in dread; and so the king was counselled by his barons not to take any landing there, but so rowed up and down the river. And the king demanded of them what they would, and said how he was come thither to speak with them, and they said all with one voice: 'We would that ye should come aland, and then we shall shew you what we lack.' Then the earl of Salisbury answered for the king and said: 'Sirs, ye be not in such order nor array that the king ought to speak with you.' And so with those words no more said: and then the king was counselled to return again to the Tower of London, and so he did.

And when these people saw that, they were inflamed with ire and returned to the hill where the great band was, and there shewed them what answer they had and how the king was returned to the Tower of London. Then they cried all with one voice, 'Let us go to London,' and so they took their way thither; and in their going they beat down abbeys and houses of advocates and of men of the court, and so came into the suburbs of London, which were great and fair, and there beat down divers fair houses, and specially they brake up the king's prisons, as the Marshalsea and other, and delivered out all the prisoners that were within: and there they did much hurt, and at the bridge foot they threat them of London because the gates of the bridge were closed, saying how they would bren all the suburbs and so conquer London by force, and to slay and bren all the commons of the city. There were many within the city of their accord, and so they drew together and said: 'Why do we not let these good people enter into the city? they are your fellows, and that that they do is for us.' So therewith the gates were opened, and then these people entered into the city and went into houses and sat down to eat and drink. They desired nothing but it was incontinent brought to them, for every man was ready to make them good cheer and to give them meat and drink to appease them.

Then the captains, as John Ball, Jack Straw and Wat Tyler, went throughout London and a twenty thousand with them, and so came to the Savoy in the way to Westminster, which was a goodly house and it pertained to the duke of Lancaster. And when they entered, they slew the keepers thereof and robbed and pilled the house, and when they had so done, then they set fire on it and clean destroyed and brent it. And when they had done that outrage, they left not therewith, but went straight to the fair hospital of the Rhodes called Saint John's,[*] and there they brent house, hospital, minster and all.

---

[*] This is called afterwards 'l'Ospital de Saint Jehan du Temple,' and therefore would probably be the Temple, to which the Hospitallers

Wat Tyler's Rebellion

Then they went from street to street and slew all the Flemings that they could find in church or in any other place, there was none respited from death. And they brake up divers houses of the Lombards and robbed them and took their goods at their pleasure, for there was none that durst say them nay. And they slew in the city a rich merchant called Richard Lyon, to whom before that time Wat Tyler had done service in France; and on a time this Richard Lyon had beaten him, while he was his varlet, the which Wat Tyler then remembered and so came to his house and stroke off his head and caused it to be borne on a spear-point before him all about the city. Thus these ungracious people demeaned themselves like people enraged and wood, and so that day they did much sorrow in London.

And so against night they went to lodge at Saint Katherine's before the Tower of London, saying how they would never depart thence till they had the king at their pleasure and till he had accorded to them all [they would ask, and] that they would ask accounts of the chancellor of England, to know where all the good was become that he had levied through the realm, and without he made a good account to them thereof, it should not be for his profit. And so when they had done all these evils to the strangers all the day, at night they lodged before the Tower.

Ye may well know and believe that it was great pity for the danger that the king and such as were with him were in. For some time these unhappy people shouted and cried so loud, as though all the devils of hell had been among them. In this evening the king was counselled by his brethren and lords and by sir Nicholas Walworth, mayor of London, and divers other notable and rich burgesses, that in the night time they should issue out of the Tower and enter into the city, and so to slay all these unhappy people, while they were at their rest and asleep;

---

had succeeded. They had, however, another house at Clerkenwell, which also had been once the property of the Templars.

for it was thought that many of them were drunken, whereby they should be slain like flies; also of twenty of them there was scant one in harness. And surely the good men of London might well have done this at their ease, for they had in their houses secretly their friends and servants ready in harness, and also sir Robert Knolles was in his lodging keeping his treasure with a sixscore ready at his commandment; in like wise was sir Perducas d'Albret, who was as then in London, insomuch that there might well [have] assembled together an eight thousand men ready in harness. Howbeit, there was nothing done, for the residue of the commons of the city were sore doubted, lest they should rise also, and the commons before were a threescore thousand or more. Then the earl of Salisbury and the wise men about the king said: 'Sir, if ye can appease them with fairness, it were best and most profitable, and to grant them everything that they desire, for if we should begin a thing the which we could not achieve, we should never recover it again, but we and our heirs ever to be disinherited.' So this counsel was taken and the mayor countermanded, and so commanded that he should not stir; and he did as he was commanded, as reason was. And in the city with the mayor there were twelve aldermen, whereof nine of them held with the king and the other three took part with these ungracious people, as it was after well known, the which they full dearly bought.

And on the Friday in the morning the people, being at Saint Katherine's near to the Tower, began to apparel themselves and to cry and shout, and said, without the king would come out and speak with them, they would assail the Tower and take it by force, and slay all them that were within. Then the king doubted these words and so was counselled that he should issue out to speak with them: and then the king sent to them that they should all draw to a fair plain place called Mile-end, whereas the people of the city did sport them in the summer season, and there the king to grant them that they desired; and there it was cried in the king's name, that whosoever would speak with the king let him go to the said place, and there he should not fail to find the king. Then the people began to depart, specially the commons of the villages, and went to the same place: but all went not thither, for they were not all of one condition; for there were some that desired nothing but riches and the utter destruction of the noblemen and to have London robbed and pilled; that was the principal matter of their beginning, the which they well shewed; for as soon as the Tower gate opened and that the king was issued out with his two brethren and the earl of Salisbury, the earl of Warwick, the earl of Oxford, sir Robert of Namur, the lord of Vertaing, the lord Gommegnies and divers other, then Wat Tyler, Jack Straw and John Ball and more than four hundred entered into the Tower and brake up chamber after chamber, and at last found the archbishop of Canterbury, called Simon, a valiant man and a wise, and chief chancellor of England, and a little before he had said mass before the king. These gluttons took him and strake off his head, and also they beheaded the lord of Saint John's and a friar minor, master in medicine, pertaining to the duke of Lancaster, they slew him in despite of his master, and a sergeant at arms called John Leg; and these four heads were set on four long spears and they made them to be borne before them through the streets of London and at last set them a-high on London bridge, as though they had been traitors to the king and to the realm. Also these gluttons entered into the princess' chamber and brake her bed, whereby she was so sore affrayed that she swooned; and there she was taken up and borne to the water side and put into a barge and covered, and so conveyed to a place called the Queen's Wardrobe;[†] and there she was all that day and night like a woman half dead, till she was comforted with the king her son, as ye shall hear after.

[†] The Queen's Wardrobe was in the 'Royal' (called by Froissart or his copyist 'la Reole'), a palace near Blackfriars.

How the nobles of England were in great peril to have been destroyed, and how these rebels were punished and sent home to their own houses

WHEN the king came to the said place of Mile-end without London, he put out of his company his two brethren, the earl of Kent and sir John Holland, and the lord of Gommegnies, for they durst not appear before the people: and when the king and his other lords were there, he found there a three-score thousand men of divers villages and of sundry countries in England; so the king entered in among them and said to them sweetly: 'Ah, ye good people, I am your king: what lack ye? what will ye say?' Then such as understood him said: 'We will that ye make us free for ever, ourselves, our heirs and our lands, and that we be called no more bond nor so reputed.' 'Sirs,' said the king, 'I am well agreed thereto. Withdraw you home into your own houses and into such villages as ye came from, and leave behind you of every village two or three, and I shall cause writings to be made and seal them with my seal, the which they shall have with them, containing everything that ye demand; and to the intent that ye shall be the better assured, I shall cause my banners to be delivered into every bailiwick, shire and countries.'

These words appeased well the common people, such as were simple and good plain men, that were come thither and wist not why. They said, 'It was well said, we desire no better.' Thus these people began to be appeased and began to withdraw

Wat Tyler's Rebellion

them into the city of London. And the king also said a word, the which greatly contented them. He said: 'Sirs, among you good men of Kent ye shall have one of my banners with you, and ye of Essex another, and ye of Sussex, of Bedford, of Cambridge, of Yarmouth, of Stafford and of Lynn, each of you one; and also I pardon everything that ye have done hitherto, so that ye follow my banners and return home to your houses.' They all answered how they would so do: thus these people departed and went into London. Then the king ordained more than thirty clerks the same Friday, to write with all diligence letter patents and sealed with the king's seal, and delivered them to these people; and when they had received the writing, they departed and returned into their own countries: but the great venom remained still behind, for Wat Tyler, Jack Straw and John Ball said, for all that these people were thus appeased, yet they would not depart so, and they had of their accord more than thirty thousand. So they abode still and made no press to have the king's writing nor seal, for all their intents was to put the city to trouble in such wise as to slay all the rich and honest persons and to rob and pill their houses. They of London were in great fear of this, wherefore they kept their houses privily with their friends and such servants as they had, every man according to his puissance. And when these said people were this Friday thus somewhat appeased, and that they should depart as soon as they had their writings, every man home into his own country, then king Richard came into the Royal, where the queen his mother was, right sore affrayed: so he comforted her as well as he could and tarried there with her all that night.

Yet I shall shew you of an adventure that fell by these ungracious people before the city of Norwich, by a captain among them called Guilliam Lister of Stafford. The same day of Corpus Christi that these people entered into London and brent the duke of Lancaster's house, called the Savoy, and the hospital of Saint John's and brake up the king's prisons and did all this hurt, as ye have heard before, the same time there assembled together they of Stafford, of Lynn, of Cambridge, of Bedford and of Yarmouth; and as they were coming towards London, they had a captain among them called Lister. And as they came, they rested them before Norwich, and in their coming they caused every man to rise with them, so that they left no villains behind them. The cause why they rested before Norwich I shall shew you. There was a knight, captain of the town, called sir Robert Sale. He was no gentleman born, but he had the grace to be reputed sage and valiant in arms, and for his valiantness king Edward made him knight. He was of his body one of the biggest knights in all England. Lister and his company thought to have had this knight with them and to make him their chief captain, to the intent to be the more feared and beloved: so they sent to him that he should come and speak with them in the field, or else they would bren the town. The knight considered that it was better for him to go and speak with them rather than they should do that outrage to the town: then he mounted on his horse and issued out of the town all alone, and so came to speak with them. And when they saw him, they made him great cheer and honoured him much, desiring him to alight off his horse and to speak with them, and so he did: wherein he did great folly; for when he was alighted, they came round about him and began to speak fair to him and said: 'Sir Robert, ye are a knight and a man greatly beloved in this country and renowned a valiant man; and though ye be thus, yet we know you well, ye be no gentleman born, but son to a villain such as we be. Therefore come you with us and be our master, and we shall make you so great a lord, that one quarter of England shall be under your obeisance.' When the knight heard them speak thus, it was greatly contrarious to his mind, for he thought never to make any such bargain, and answered them with a felonous regard: 'Fly away, ye ungracious people, false and evil traitors that ye be: would you that I should forsake my natural lord for such a company of knaves as ye be, to my dishonour for ever? I had rather ye were all hanged, as ye shall be; for that shall be your end.' And with those words he had thought to have leapt again upon his horse, but he failed of the stirrup and the horse started away. Then they cried all at him and said: 'Slay him without mercy.' When he heard those words, he let his horse go and drew out a good sword and began to scrimmish* with them, and made a great place about him, that it was pleasure to behold him. There was none that durst approach near him: there were some that approached near him, but at every stroke that he gave he cut off other leg, head or arm: there was none so hardy but that they feared him: he did there such deeds of arms that it was marvel to regard. But there were more than forty thousand of these unhappy people: they shot and cast at him, and he was unarmed: to say truth, if he had been of iron or steel, yet he must needs have been slain; but yet, or he died, he slew twelve out of hand, beside them that he hurt. Finally he was stricken to the earth, and they cut off his arms and legs and then strake his body all to pieces. This was the end of sir Robert Sale, which was great damage; for which deed afterward all the knights and squires of England were angry and sore displeased when they heard thereof.

Now let us return to the king. The Saturday the king departed from the Wardrobe in the Royal and went to Westminster and heard mass in the church there, and all his lords with him. And beside the church there was a little chapel with an image of our Lady, which did great miracles and in whom the kings of England had ever great trust and confidence. The king made his orisons before this image and did there his offering; and then he leapt on his horse, and all his lords, and so the king rode toward London; and when he had ridden a little way, on the left hand there was a way to pass without London.†

The same proper morning Wat Tyler, Jack Straw and John Ball had assembled their company to common together in a place called Smithfield, whereas every Friday there is a market of horses; and there were together all of affinity more than

---

* scrimmish = skirmish

† Or rather, 'he found a place on the left hand to pass without London.'

twenty thousand, and yet there were many still in the town, drinking and making merry in the taverns and paid nothing, for they were happy that made them best cheer. And these people in Smithfield had with them the king's banners, the which were delivered them the day before, and all these gluttons were in mind to overrun and to rob London the same day; for their captains said how they had done nothing as yet. 'These liberties that the king hath given us is to us but a small profit: therefore let us be all of one accord and let us overrun this rich and puissant city, or they of Essex, of Sussex, of Cambridge, of Bedford, of Arundel, of Warwick, of Reading, of Oxford, of Guildford, of Lynn, of Stafford, of Yarmouth, of Lincoln, of York and of Durham do come hither. For all these will come hither; Baker and Lister will bring them hither; and if we be first lords of London and have the possession of the riches that is therein, we shall not repent us; for if we leave it, they that come after will have it from us.'

To this counsel they all agreed; and therewith the king came the same way unware of them, for he had thought to have passed that way without London, and with him a forty horse. And when he came before the abbey of Saint Bartholomew and beheld all these people, then the king rested and said how he would go no farther till he knew what these people ailed, saying, if they were in any trouble, how he would rappease them again. The lords that were with him tarried also, as reason was when they saw the king tarry. And when Wat Tyler saw the king tarry, he said to his people: 'Sirs, yonder is the king: I will go and speak with him. Stir not from hence, without I make you a sign; and when I make you that sign, come on and slay all them except the king; but do the king no hurt, he is young, we shall do with him as we list and shall lead him with us all about England, and so shall we be lords of all the realm without doubt.' And there was a doublet-maker of London called John Tycle, and he had brought to these gluttons a sixty doublets, the which they ware: then he demanded of these captains who should pay him for his doublets; he demanded thirty mark. Wat Tyler answered him and said: 'Friend, appease yourself, thou shalt be well paid or this day be ended. Keep thee near me; I shall be thy creditor.' And therewith he spurred his horse and departed from his company and came to the king, so near him that his horse head touched the croup of the king's horse, and the first word that he said was this: 'Sir king, seest thou all yonder people?' 'Yea truly,' said the king, 'wherefore sayest thou?' 'Because,' said he, 'they be all at my commandment and have sworn to me faith and truth, to do all that I will have them.' 'In a good time,' said the king, 'I will well it be so.' Then Wat Tyler said, as he that nothing demanded but riot: 'What believest thou, king, that these people and as many more as be in London at my commandment, that they will depart from thee thus without having thy letters? ' 'No,' said the king, 'ye shall have them: they be ordained for you and shall be delivered every one each after other. Wherefore, good fellows, withdraw fair and easily to your people and cause them to depart out of London; for it is our intent that each of you by villages and townships shall have letters patents, as I have promised you.'

With those words Wat Tyler cast his eyen on a squire that was there with the king bearing the king's sword, and Wat Tyler hated greatly the same squire, for the same squire had displeased him before for words between them. 'What, said Tyler, 'art thou there? Give me thy dagger.' 'Nay,' said the squire, 'that will I not do: wherefore should I give it thee?' The king beheld the squire and said: 'Give it him; let him have it.' And so the squire took it him sore against his will. And when this Wat Tyler had it, he began to play therewith and turned it in his hand, and said again to the squire: 'Give me also that sword.' 'Nay,' said the squire, 'it is the king's sword: thou art not worthy to have it, for thou art but a knave; and if there were no more here but thou and I, thou durst not speak those words for as much gold in quantity as all yonder abbey.'[‡] 'By my faith,' said

---

[‡] The full text has, 'for as much gold as that minster of Saint Paul is great.'

Wat Tyler, 'I shall never eat meat till I have thy head': and with those words the mayor of London came to the king with a twelve horses well armed under their coats, and so he brake the press and saw and heard how Wat Tyler demeaned himself, and said to him: 'Ha, thou knave, how art thou so hardy in the king's presence to speak such words? It is too much for thee so to do.' Then the king began to chafe and said to the mayor: 'Set hands on him.' And while the king said so, Tyler said to the mayor: 'A God's name what have I said to displease thee?' 'Yes truly,' quoth the mayor, 'thou false stinking knave, shalt thou speak thus in the presence of the king my natural lord? I commit never to live, without thou shalt dearly abye it.'[§] And with those words the mayor drew out his sword and strake Tyler so great a stroke on the head, that he fell down at the feet of his horse, and as soon as he was fallen, they environed him all about, whereby he was not seen of his company. Then a squire of the king's alighted, called John Standish, and he drew out his sword and put it into Wat Tyler's belly, and so he died.

Then the ungracious people there assembled, perceiving their captain slain, began to murmur among themselves and said: 'Ah, our captain is slain, let us go and slay them all': and therewith they arranged themselves on the place in manner of battle, and their bows before them. Thus the king began a great outrage;[**] howbeit, all turned to the best: for as soon as Tyler was on the earth, the king departed from all his company and all alone he rode to these people, and said to his own men: 'Sirs, none of you follow me; let me alone.' And so when he came before these ungracious people, who put themselves in ordinance to revenge their captain, then the king said to them: 'Sirs, what aileth you? Ye shall have no captain but me: I am your king: be all in rest and peace.' And so the most part of the people that

---

[§] 'Jamais je veux vivre, si tu ne le compares.'

[**] 'Outrage' here means 'act of boldness,' as elsewhere, e. g. 'si fist une grant apertisee d'armes et un grant outrage.'

Wat Tyler's Rebellion

heard the king speak and saw him among them, were shamefast and began to wax peaceable and to depart; but some, such as were malicious and evil, would not depart, but made semblant as though they would do somewhat.

Then the king returned to his own company and demanded of them what was best to be done. Then he was counselled to draw into the field, for to fly away was no boot. Then said the mayor: 'It is good that we do so, for I think surely we shall have shortly some comfort of them of London and of such good men as be of our part, who are purveyed and have their friends and men ready armed in their houses.' And in the mean time voice and bruit ran through London how these unhappy people were likely to slay the king and the mayor in Smithfield; through the which noise all manner of good men of the king's party issued out of their houses and lodgings well armed, and so came all to Smithfield and to the field where the king was, and they were anon to the number of seven or eight thousand men well armed. And first thither came sir Robert Knolles and sir Perducas d'Albret, well accompanied, and divers of the aldermen of London, and with them a six hundred men in harness, and a puissant man of the city, who was the king's draper,[††] called Nicholas Bramber, and he brought with him a great company; and ever as they came, they ranged them afoot in order of battle: and on the other part these unhappy people were ready ranged, making semblance to give battle, and they had with them divers of the king's banners. There the king made three knights, the one the mayor of London sir Nicholas Walworth, sir John Standish and sir Nicholas Bramber. Then the lords said among themselves: 'What shall we do? We see here our enemies, who would gladly slay us, if they might have the better hand of us.' Sir Robert Knolles counselled to go and fight with them and slay them all; yet the king would not consent

---

[††] 'Qui estoit des draps du roy.' He owned large estates in Essex and also shops in London. He became one of the councillors of Richard II.

thereto, but said: 'Nay, I will not so: I will send to them commanding them to send me again my banners, and thereby we shall see what they will do. Howbeit, other by fairness or otherwise, I will have them.' 'That is well said, sir,' quoth the earl of Salisbury. Then these new knights were sent to them, and these knights made token to them not to shoot at them, and when they came so near them that their speech might be heard, they said: 'Sirs, the king commandeth you to send to him again his banners, and we think he will have mercy of you.' And incontinent they delivered again the banners and sent them to the king. Also they were commanded on pain of their heads, that all such as had letters of the king to bring them forth and to send them again to the king; and so many of them delivered their letters, but not all. Then the king made them to be all to-torn in their presence; and as soon as the king's banners were delivered again, these unhappy people kept none array, but the most part of them did cast down their bows, and so brake their array and returned into London. Sir Robert Knolles was sore displeased in that he might not go to slay them all: but the king would not consent thereto, but said he would be revenged of them well enough; and so he was after.

Thus these foolish people departed, some one way and some another; and the king and his lords and all his company right ordinately entered into London with great joy. And the first journey that the king made he went to the lady princess his mother, who was in a castle in the Royal called the Queen's Wardrobe, and there she had tarried two days and two nights right sore abashed, as she had good reason; and when she saw the king her son, she was greatly rejoiced and said: 'Ah, fair son, what pain and great sorrow that I have suffered for you this day!' Then the king answered and said: 'Certainly, madam, I know it well; but now rejoice yourself and thank God, for now it is time. I have this day recovered mine heritage and the realm of England, the which I had near lost.' Thus the king tarried that day with his mother, and every lord went peaceably to their own lodgings. Then there was a cry made in every street in the king's

Wat Tyler's Rebellion

name, that all manner of men, not being of the city of London and have not dwelt there the space of one year, to depart; and if any such be found there the Sunday by the sun-rising, that they should be taken as traitors to the king and to lose their heads. This cry thus made, there was none that durst brake it, and so all manner of people departed and sparkled abroad every man to their own places. John Ball and Jack Straw were found in an old house hidden, thinking to have stolen away, but they could not, for they were accused by their own men. Of the taking of them the king and his lords were glad, and then strake off their heads and Wat Tyler's also, and they were set on London bridge, and the valiant men's heads taken down that they had set on the Thursday before. These tidings anon spread abroad, so that the people of the strange countries, which were coming towards London, returned back again to their own houses and durst come no farther. .

Chapter 4
The Battle of Otterburn

How the Earl Douglas won the pennon of Sir Henry Percy at the barriers before Newcastle-upon-Tyne, and how the Scots brent the Castle of Pontland, and how Sir Henry Percy and Sir Ralph his Brother took advice to follow the Scots to conquer again the pennon that was lost at the scrimmish

WHEN the English lords saw that their squire returned not again at the time appointed, and could know nothing what the Scots did, nor what they were purposed to do, then they thought well that their squire was taken. The lords sent each to other, to be ready whensoever they should hear that the Scots were abroad: as for their messenger, they thought him but lost.

Now let us speak of the earl Douglas and other, for they had more to do than they that went by Carlisle. When the earls of Douglas, of Moray, of March, and Dunbar[*] departed from the great host, they took their way thinking to pass the water and to enter into the bishopric of Durham, and to ride to the town and then to return, brenning and exiling the country and so to come to Newcastle and to lodge there in the town in the despite of all the Englishmen. And as they determined, so they did assay to put it in use, for they rode a great pace under covert without doing of any pillage by the way or assaulting of any castle, tower

---

[*] George, earl of March and Dunbar: the text gives Mare, but there was at this time no earl of Mar.

or house, but so came into the lord Percy's land and passed the river of Tyne without any let a three leagues above Newcastle not far from Brancepeth, and at last entered into the bishopric of Durham, where they found a good country. Then they began to make war, to slay people and to bren villages and to do many sore displeasures.

As at that time the earl of Northumberland and the other lords and knights of that country knew nothing of their coming. When tidings came to Newcastle and to Durham that the Scots were abroad, and that they might well see by the fires and smoke abroad in the country, the earl sent to Newcastle his two sons and sent commandment to every man to draw to Newcastle, saying to his sons: 'Ye shall go to Newcastle and all the country shall assemble there, and I shall tarry at Alnwick, which is a passage that they must pass by. If we may enclose them, we shall speed well.' Sir Henry Percy and sir Ralph his brother obeyed their father's commandment and came thither with them of the country. The Scots rode burning and exiling the country, that the smoke thereof came to Newcastle. The Scots came to the gates of Durham and scrimmished there; but they tarried not long but returned, as they had ordained before to do, and that they found by the way took and destroyed it. Between Durham and Newcastle is but twelve leagues English and a good country: there was no town, without it were closed, but it was brent, and they repassed the river of Tyne where they had passed before, and then came before Newcastle and there rested. All the English knights and squires of the country of York and bishopric of Durham were assembled at Newcastle, and thither came the seneschal of York, sir Ralph Lumley, sir Matthew Redman, captain of Berwick, sir Robert Ogle, sir Thomas Grey, sir Thomas Holton, sir John Felton, sir John Lilleburn, sir Thomas Abingdon, the baron of Hilton, sir John Coppledike and divers other, so that the town was so full of people that they wist not where to lodge.

The Battle of Otterburn

When these three Scottish earls who were chief captains had made their enterprise in the bishopric of Durham and had sore overrun the country, then they returned to Newcastle and there rested and tarried two days, and every day they scrimmished. The earl of Northumberland's two sons were two young lusty knights and were ever foremost at the barriers to scrimmish. There were many proper feats of arms done and achieved: there was fighting hand to hand: among other there fought hand to hand the earl Douglas and sir Henry Percy, and by force of arms the earl Douglas won the pennon of sir Henry Percy's, wherewith he was sore displeased and so were all the Englishmen. And the earl Douglas said to sir Henry Percy: 'Sir, I shall bear this token of your prowess into Scotland and shall set it on high on my castle of Dalkeith, that it may be seen far off.' 'Sir,' quoth sir Henry, 'ye may be sure ye shall not pass the bounds of this country till ye be met withal in such wise that ye shall make none avaunt[†] thereof.' 'Well, sir,' quoth the earl Douglas, 'come this night to my lodging and seek for your pennon: I shall set it before my lodging and see if ye will come to take it away.' So then it was late, and the Scots withdrew to their lodgings and refreshed them with such as they had. They had flesh enough: they made that night good watch, for they thought surely to be awaked for the words they had spoken, but they were not, for sir Henry Percy was counselled not so to do.

The next day the Scots dislodged and returned towards their own country, and so came to a castle and a town called Pontland, whereof sir Edmund of Alphel was lord, who was a right good knight. There the Scots rested, for they came thither betimes, and understood that the knight was in his castle. Then they ordained to assail the castle, and gave a great assault, so that by force of arms they won it and the knight within it. Then the town and castle was brent; and from thence the Scots went to

---

[†] avaunt = depart.

The Chronicles of Froissart

the town and castle of Otterburn,‡ an eight English mile from Newcastle§ and there lodged. That day they made none assault, but the next morning they blew their horns and made ready to assail the castle, which was strong, for it stood in the marish**. That day they assaulted till they were weary, and did nothing. Then they sowned the retreat and returned to their lodgings. Then the lords drew to council to determine what they should do. The most part were of the accord that the next day they should dislodge without giving of any assault and to draw fair and easily towards Carlisle. But the earl Douglas brake that counsel and said: 'In despite of sir Henry Percy, who said he would come and win again his pennon, let us not depart hence for two or three days. Let us assail this castle: it is pregnable: we shall have double honour. And then let us see if he will come and fetch his pennon: he shall be well defended.'†† Every man accorded to his saying, what for their honour and for the love of him. Also they lodged there at their ease, for there was none that troubled them: they made many lodgings of boughs and great herbs and fortified their camp sagely with the marish that was thereby, and their carriages were set at the entry into the

---

‡

§ Froissart says 'eight English leagues.' In the next chapter the distance becomes 'seven little leagues,' and later on, 'a six English miles,' where the original is 'lieues.' The actual distance is about thirty miles. The translator gives the form 'Combur' here. but 'Ottenburge' in the next chapter, as the name of the place. It is remarkable indeed how little trouble he seems to have taken generally to give English names correctly. In this chapter we have 'Nymyche' for 'Alnwick' and 'Pouclan' for 'Pontland,' forms rather less like the real names than those which he found in the French text, viz. Nynich and Ponclau.

** marish = marsh.

†† Froissart says, 'if he comes, it shall be defended.' The translator perhaps means 'he shall be prevented.'

The Battle of Otterburn

marishes and had all their beasts within the marish. Then they apparelled for to assault the next day: this was their intention.

Now let us speak of sir Henry Percy and of sir Ralph his brother and shew somewhat what they did. They were sore displeased that the earl Douglas had won the pennon of their arms: also it touched greatly their honours, if they did not as sir Henry Percy said he would; for he had said to the earl Douglas that he should not carry his pennon out of England, and also he had openly spoken it before all the knights and squires that were at Newcastle. The Englishmen there thought surely that the earl Douglas' band was but the Scots' vanguard and that their host was left behind. The knights of the country, such as were well expert in arms, spake against sir Henry Percy's opinion and said to him: 'Sir, there fortuneth in war oftentimes many losses. If the earl Douglas have won your pennon, he bought it dear, for he came to the gate to seek it and was well beaten:‡‡ another day ye shall win as much of him or more. Sir, we say this because we know well all the power of Scotland is abroad in the fields, and if we issue out and be not men enow to fight with them, and peradventure they have made this scrimmish with us to the intent to draw us out of the town, and the number that they be of, as it is said, above forty thousand men, they may soon enclose us and do with us what they will. Yet it were better to lose a pennon than two or three hundred knights and squires and put all our country in adventure.' These words refrained sir Henry and his brother, for they would do nothing against counsel. Then tidings came to them by such as had seen the Scots and seen all their demeanour and what way they took and where they rested.

---

‡‡ i. e. 'well fought with.'

How Sir Henry Percy and his brother with a good number of men of arms and archers went after the Scots, to win again his pennon that the Earl Douglas had won before Newcastle-upon-Tyne, and how they assailed the Scots before Otterburn in their lodgings

IT was shewed to sir Henry Percy and to his brother and to the other knights and squires that were there, by such as had followed the Scots from Newcastle and had well advised their doing, who said to sir Henry and to sir Ralph: 'Sirs, we have followed the Scots privily and have discovered all the country. The Scots be at Pontland and have taken sir Edmund Alphel in his own castle, and from thence they be gone to Otterburn and there they lay this night. What they will do to-morrow we know not: they are ordained to abide there: and, sirs, surely their great host is not with them, for in all they pass not there a three thousand men.' When sir Henry heard that, he was joyful and said: 'Sirs, let us leap on our horses, for by the faith I owe to God and to my lord my father I will go seek for my pennon and dislodge them this same night.' Knights and squires that heard him agreed thereto and were joyous, and every man made him ready.

The same evening the bishop of Durham came thither with a good company, for he heard at Durham how the Scots were before Newcastle and how that the lord Percy's sons with other lords and knights should fight with the Scots: therefore the

The Battle of Otterburn

bishop of Durham to come to the rescue had assembled up all the country and so was coming to Newcastle. But sir Henry Percy would not abide his coming, for he had with him six hundred spears, knights and squires, and an eight thousand footmen. They thought that sufficient number to fight with the Scots, if they were not but three hundred spears and three thousand of other. Thus they departed from Newcastle after dinner and set forth in good order, and took the same way as the Scots had gone and rode to Otterburn, a seven little leagues from thence and fair way, but they could not ride fast because of their foot-men. And when the Scots had supped and some laid down to their rest, and were weary of travailing and assaulting of the castle all that day, and thought to rise early in the morning in cool of the day to give a new assault, therewith suddenly the Englishmen came on them and entered into the lodgings, weening it had been the masters' lodgings, and therein were but varlets and servants. Then the Englishmen cried, 'Percy, Percy!' and entered into the lodgings, and ye know well where such affray is noise is soon raised: and it fortuned well for the Scots, for when they saw the Englishmen came to wake them, then the lord sent a certain of their servants of foot-men to scrimmish with the Englishmen at the entry of the lodgings, and in the mean time they armed and apparelled them, every man under his banner and under his captain's pennon. The night was far on, but the moon shone so bright as an it had been in a manner day. It was in the month of August and the weather fair and temperate.

Thus the Scots were drawn together and without any noise departed from their lodgings and went about a little mountain, which was greatly for their advantage. For all the day before they had well advised the place and said among themselves: 'If the Englishmen come on us suddenly, then we will do thus and thus, for it is a jeopardous thing in the night if men of war enter into our lodgings. If they do, then we will draw to such a place, and thereby other we shall win or lose.' When the Englishmen entered into the field, at the first they soon overcame the varlets, and as they entered further in, always they found new men to busy them and to scrimmish with them. Then suddenly came the Scots from about the mountain and set on the Englishmen or they were ware, and cried their cries; whereof the Englishmen were sore astonied. Then they cried 'Percy!' and the other party cried 'Douglas!'

There began a cruel battle and at the first encounter many were overthrown of both parties; and because the Englishmen were a great number and greatly desired to vanquish their enemies, and rested at their pace[*] and greatly did put aback the Scots, so that the Scots were near discomfited. Then the earl James Douglas, who was young and strong and of great desire to get praise and grace, and was willing to deserve to have it, and cared for no pain nor travail, came forth with his banner and cried, 'Douglas, Douglas!' and sir Henry Percy and sir Ralph his brother, who had great indignation against the earl Douglas because he had won the pennon of their arms at the barriers before Newcastle, came to that part and cried, 'Percy!' Their two banners met and their men: there was a sore fight: the Englishmen were so strong and fought so valiantly that they reculed[†] the Scots back. There were two valiant knights of Scots under the banner of the earl Douglas, called sir Patrick of Hepbourn and sir Patrick his son. They acquitted themselves that day valiantly: the earl's banner had been won, an they had not been: they defended it so valiantly and in the rescuing thereof did such feats of arms, that it was greatly to their recommendation and to their heirs' for ever after.

It was shewed me by such as had been at the same battle, as well by knights and squires of England as of Scotland, at the house of the earl of Foix, -- for anon after this battle was done I met at Orthez two squires of England called John of Chateauneuf and John of Cantiron; also when I returned to

---

[*] In French, 'ilz se arresterent,' without 'and.'

[†] recule (as transitive) = repulse

The Battle of Otterburn

Avignon I found also there a knight and a squire of Scotland; I knew them and they knew me by such tokens as I shewed them of their country, for I, author of this book, in my youth had ridden nigh over all the realm of Scotland, and I was as then a fifteen days in the house of earl William Douglas, father to the same earl James, of whom I spake of now, in a castle of five leagues from Edinburgh in the country, of Dalkeith;[‡] the same time I saw there this earl James, a fair young child, and a sister of his called the lady Blanche, -- and I was informed by both these parties[§] how this battle was as sore a battle fought as lightly hath been heard of before of such a number; and I believe it well, for Englishmen on the one party and Scots on the other party are good men of war, for when they meet there is a hard fight without sparing, there is no ho between them as long as spears, swords, axes or daggers will endure, but lay on each upon other, and when they be well beaten[**] and that the one party hath obtained the victory, they then glorify so in their deeds of arms and are so joyful, that such as be taken they shall be ransomed or they go out of the field, so that shortly each of them is so content with other that at their departing courteously they will say, 'God thank you'; but in fighting one with another there is no play nor sparing, and this is true, and that shall well appear by this said rencounter, for it was as valiantly foughten as could be devised, as ye shall hear.

[‡] 'Which is called in the country Dalkeith.' The French has 'que on nomme au pays Dacquest,' of which the translator makes 'in the countrey of Alquest.'

[§] By both sides,' i. e. Scotch and English.

[**] 'When they have well fought.'

How the Earl James Douglas by his valiantness encouraged his men, who were reculed and in a manner discomfited, and in his so doing he was wounded to death

KNIGHTS and squires were of good courage on both parties to fight valiantly: cowards there had no place, but hardiness reigned with goodly feats of arms, for knights and squires were so joined together at hand strokes, that archers had no place of nother party. There the Scots shewed great hardiness and fought merrily with great desire of honour: the Englishmen were three to one: howbeit, I say not but Englishmen did nobly acquit themselves, for ever the Englishmen had rather been slain or taken in the place than to fly. Thus, as I have said, the banners of Douglas and Percy and their men were met each against other, envious who should win the honour of that journey. At the beginning the Englishmen were so strong that they reculed back their enemies: then the earl Douglas, who was of great heart and high of enterprise, seeing his men recule back, then to recover the place and to shew knightly valour he took his axe in both his hands, and entered so into the press that he made himself way in such wise, that none durst approach near him, and he was so well armed that he bare well off such strokes as he received.*
Thus he went ever forward like a hardy Hector, willing alone to conquer the field and to discomfit his enemies: but at last he was encountered with three spears all at once, the one strake him on

---

* 'No man was so well armed that he did not fear the great strokes which he gave.'

The Battle of Otterburn

the shoulder, the other on the breast and the stroke glinted down to his belly, and the third strake him in the thigh, and sore hurt with all three strokes, so that he was borne perforce to the earth and after that he could not be again relieved. Some of his knights and squires followed him, but not all, for it was night, and no light but by the shining of the moon. The Englishmen knew well they had borne one down to the earth, but they wist not who it was; for if they had known that it had been the earl Douglas, they had been thereof so joyful and so proud that the victory had been theirs. Nor also the Scots knew not of that adventure till the end of the battle; for if they had known it, they should have been so sore despaired and discouraged that they would have fled away. Thus as the earl Douglas was felled to the earth, he was stricken into the head with an axe, and another stroke through the thigh: the Englishmen passed forth and took no heed of him: they thought none otherwise but that they had slain a man of arms. On the other part the earl George de la March and of Dunbar fought right valiantly and gave the Englishmen much ado, and cried, 'Follow Douglas,' and set on the sons of Percy: also earl John of Moray with his banner and men fought valiantly and set fiercely on the Englishmen, and gave them so much to do that they wist not to whom to attend.

How in this Battle Sir Ralph Percy was sore hurt and taken prisoner by a Scottish knight

OF all the battles and encounterings that I have made mention of herebefore in all this history, great or small, this battle that I treat of now was one of the sorest and best foughten without cowardice or faint hearts. For there was nother knight nor squire but that did his devoir and fought hand to hand: this battle was like the battle of Becherel,[*] the which was valiantly fought and endured. The earl of Northumberland's sons, sir Henry and sir Ralph Percy, who were chief sovereign captains, acquitted themselves nobly, and sir Ralph Percy entered in so far among his enemies that he was closed in and hurt, and so sore handled that his breath was so short, that he was taken prisoner by a knight of the earl of Moray's called sir John Maxwell. In the taking the Scottish knight demanded what he was, for it was in the night, so that he knew him not, and sir Ralph was so sore overcome and bled fast, that at last he said: 'I am Ralph Percy.' Then the Scot said: 'Sir Ralph, rescue or no rescue I take you for my prisoner: I am Maxwell.' 'Well,' quoth sir Ralph, 'I am content: but then take heed to me, for I am sore hurt, my hosen and my greaves are full of blood.' Then the knight saw by him the earl Moray and said: 'Sir, here I deliver to you sir Ralph Percy as prisoner; but, sir, let good heed be taken to him, for he is sore hurt.' The earl was joyful of these words and said: 'Maxwell, thou hast well won thy spurs.' Then he delivered sir Ralph Percy to certain of his men, and they stopped and wrapped his wounds: and still the battle endured, not knowing who had as

---

[*] Or, according to another reading, 'Cocherel.'

The Battle of Otterburn

then the better, for there were many taken and rescued again that came to no knowledge.

Now let us speak of the young James earl of Douglas, who did marvels in arms or he was beaten down. When he was overthrown, the press was great about him, so that he could not relieve, for with an axe he had his death's wound. His men followed him as near as they could, and there came to him sir James Lindsay his cousin and sir John and sir Walter Sinclair and other knights and squires. And by him was a gentle knight of his, who followed him all the day, and a chaplain of his, not like a priest but like a valiant man of arms, for all that night he followed the earl with a good axe in his hands and still scrimmished about the earl there as he lay, and reculed back some of the Englishmen with great strokes that he gave. Thus he was found fighting near to his master, whereby he had great praise, and thereby the same year he was made archdeacon of Aberdeen. This priest was called sir William of North Berwick: he was a tall man and a hardy and was sore hurt. When these knights came to the earl, they found him in an evil case and a knight of his lying by him called sir Robert Hart: he had a fifteen wounds in one place and other. Then sir John Sinclair demanded of the earl how he did. 'Right evil, cousin,' quoth the earl, 'but thanked be God there hath been but a few of mine ancestors that hath died in their beds: but, cousin, I require you think to revenge me, for I reckon myself but dead, for my heart fainteth oftentimes. My cousin Walter and you, I pray you raise up again my banner which lieth on the ground, and my squire Davie Collemine slain: but, sirs, shew nother to friend nor foe in what case ye see me in; for if mine enemies knew it, they would rejoice, and our friends discomforted.' The two brethren of Sinclair and sir James Lindsay did as the earl had desired them and raised up again his banner and cried 'Douglas!' Such as were behind and heard that cry drew together and set on their enemies valiantly and reculed back the Englishmen and many overthrown, and so drave the Englishmen back beyond the place whereas the earl lay, who was by that time dead, and so came to the earl's banner, the which sir John Sinclair held in his hands, and many good knights and squires of Scotland about him, and still company drew to the cry of 'Douglas.' Thither came the earl Moray with his banner well accompanied, and also the earl de la March and of Dunbar, and when they saw the Englishmen recule and their company assembled together, they renewed again the battle and gave many hard and sad strokes.

How the Scots won the Battle against the Englishmen beside Otterburn, and there was taken prisoners Sir Henry and Sir Ralph Percy, and how an English squire would not yield him, no more would a Scottish squire, and so died both; and how the Bishop of Durham and his company were discomfited among themselves

To say truth, the Englishmen were sorer travailed than the Scots, for they came the same day from Newcastle-upon-Tyne, a six English miles, and went a great pace to the intent to find the Scots, which they did; so that by their fast going they were near out of breath, and the Scots were fresh and well rested, which greatly availed them when time was of their business: for in the last scrimmish they reculed back the Englishmen in such wise, that after that they could no more assemble together, for the Scots passed through their battles. And it fortuned that sir Henry Percy and the lord of Montgomery, a valiant knight of Scotland, fought together hand to hand right valiantly without letting of any other, for every man had enough to do. So long they two fought that per force of arms sir Henry Percy was taken prisoner by the said lord of Montgomery.

The knights and squires of Scotland, as sir Marc Adreman,* sir Thomas Erskine, sir William, sir James and sir Alexander Lindsay, the lord of Fenton, sir John of Saint-Moreaulx,† sir Patrick of Dunbar, sir John and sir Walter Sinclair, sir John Maxwell, sir Guy Stuart, sir John Haliburton, sir Alexander Ramsay, Robert Collemine‡ and his two sons John and Robert; who were there made knights, and a hundred knights and squires that I cannot name, all these right valiantly did acquit themselves. And on the English party, before that the lord Percy was taken and after, there fought valiantly sir Ralph Lumley, sir Matthew Redman, sir Thomas Ogle, sir Thomas Gray, sir Thomas Helton, sir Thomas Abingdon, sir John Lilleburn, sir William Walsingham, the baron of Helton, sir John of Colpedich,§ the seneschal of York and divers other footmen. Whereto should I write long process? This was a sore battle and well foughten; and as fortune is always changeable, though the Englishmen were more in number than the Scots and were right valiant men of war and well expert, and that at the first front they reculed back the Scots, yet finally the Scots obtained the place and victory, and all the foresaid Englishmen taken, and a hundred more, saving sir Matthew Redman, captain of Berwick, who when he knew no remedy nor recoverance, and saw his company fly from the Scots and yielded them on every side, then he took his horse and departed to save himself.

The same season about the end of this discomfiture there was an English squire called Thomas Waltham, a goodly and a valiant man, and that was well seen, for of all that night he would nother fly nor yet yield him. It was said he had made a vow at a feast in England, that the first time that ever he saw

---

* Perhaps 'Malcolm Drummond.'
† The true reading seems to be 'Sandilands.'
‡ Perhaps 'Coningham.'
§ Either 'Copeland' or 'Copeldike.'

Englishmen and Scots in battle, he would so do his devoir[**] to his power, in such wise that either he would be reputed for the best doer on both sides or else to die in the pain. He was called a valiant and a hardy man and did so much by his prowess, that under the banner of the earl of Moray he did such valiantness in arms, that the Scots had marvel thereof, and so was slain in fighting: the Scots would gladly have taken him alive, but he would never yield, he hoped ever to have been rescued. And with him there was a Scottish squire slain, cousin to the king of Scots, called Simon Glendowyn; his death was greatly complained of the Scots.

This battle was fierce and cruel till it came to the end of the discomfiture; but when the Scots saw the Englishmen recule and yield themselves, then the Scots were courteous and set them to their ransom, and every man said to his prisoner: 'Sirs, go and unarm you and take your ease; I am your master:' and so made their prisoners as good cheer as though they had been brethren, without doing to them any damage. The chase endured a five English miles, and if the Scots had been men enow, there had none scaped, but other they had been taken or slain. And if Archambault Douglas and the earl of Fife, the earl Sutherland and other of the great company who were gone towards Carlisle had been there, by all likelihood they had taken the bishop of Durham and the town of Newcastle-upon-Tyne. I shall shew you how. The same evening that the Percies departed from Newcastle, as ye have heard before, the bishop of Durham with the rearband came to Newcastle and supped: and as he sat at the table, he had imagination in himself how he did not acquit himself well to see the Englishmen in the field and he to be within the town. Incontinent he caused the table to be taken away and commanded to saddle his horses and to sown the trumpets, and called up men in the town to arm themselves and to mount on their horses, and foot-men to order themselves to depart. And thus every man departed out of the town to the

---

[**] devoir = duty

number of seven thousand, two thousand on horseback and five thousand afoot; they took their way toward Otterburn, whereas the battle had been. And by that time they had gone two mile [††] from Newcastle tidings came to them how their men were fighting with the Scots. Therewith the bishop rested there, and incontinent came more flying fast, that they were out of breath. Then they were demanded how the matter went. They answered and said: 'Right evil; we be all discomfited: here cometh the Scots chasing of us.' These tidings troubled the Englishmen, and began to doubt. And again the third time men came flying as fast as they might. When the men of the bishopric of Durham heard of these evil tidings, they were abashed in such wise that they brake their array, so that the bishop could not hold together the number of five hundred. It was thought that if the Scots had followed them in any number, seeing that it was night, that in the entering into the town, and the Englishmen so abashed, the town had been won.

The bishop of Durham, being in the field, had good will to have succoured the Englishmen and recomforted his men as much as he could; but he saw his own men fly as well as other. Then he demanded counsel of sir William Lucy and of sir Thomas Clifford and of other knights, what was best to do. These knights for their honour would give him no counsel; for they thought to return again and do nothing should sown greatly to their blame, and to go forth might be to their great damage; and so stood still and would give none answer, and the longer they stood, the fewer they were, for some still stale away. Then the bishop said: 'Sirs, all things considered, it is none honour to put all in peril, nor to make of one evil damage twain. We hear how our company be discomfited, and we cannot remedy it: for to go to recover them, we know not with whom nor with what number we shall meet. Let us return fair and easily for this night to Newcastle, and to-morrow let us draw together and go look on our enemies.' Every man answered: 'As God will, so be it.'

[††] The word 'lieue' is translated 'mile' throughout.

The Battle of Otterburn

Therewith they returned to Newcastle. Thus a man may consider the great default that is in men that be abashed and discomfited: for if they had kept them together and have turned again such as fled, they had discomfited the Scots. This was the opinion of divers; and because they did not thus, the Scots had the victory.

How Sir Matthew Redman departed from the Battle to save himself; and how Sir James Lindsay was taken prisoner by the Bishop of Durham; and how after the Battle scurrers[*] were sent forth to discover the country

I SHALL shew you of sir Matthew Redman, who was on horseback to save himself, for he alone could not remedy the matter. At his departing sir James Lindsay was near to him and saw how sir Matthew departed, and this sir James, to win honour, followed in chase sir Matthew Redman, and came so near him that he might have striken him with his spear, if he had list. Then he said: 'Ah, sir knight, turn; it is a shame thus to fly: I am James of Lindsay: if ye will not turn, I shall strike you on the back with my spear.' Sir Matthew spake no word, but strake his horse with the spurs sorer than he did before. In this manner he chased him more than three miles, and at last sir Matthew Redman's horse foundered and fell under him. Then he stept forth on the earth and drew out his sword, and took courage to defend himself; and the Scot thought to have stricken him on the breast, but sir Matthew Redman swerved from the stroke, and the spear-point entered into the earth. Then sir Matthew strake asunder the spear with his sword; and when sir James Lindsay saw how he had lost his spear, he cast away the truncheon and lighted afoot, and took a little battle-axe that he carried at his back and handled it with his one hand quickly and deliverly, in the which feat Scots be well expert, and then he set at sir

---

[*] scurrer = scout.

The Battle of Otterburn

Matthew and he defended himself properly. Thus they tourneyed together, one with an axe and the other with a sword, a long season, and no man to let them. Finally sir James Lindsay gave the knight such strokes and held him so short, that he was put out of breath in such wise that he yielded himself, and said: 'Sir James Lindsay, I yield me to you.' 'Well,' quoth he, 'and I receive you, rescue or no rescue.' 'I am content,' quoth Redman, 'so ye deal with me like a good companion.' 'I shall not fail that,' quoth Lindsay, and so put up his sword. 'Well, sir,' quoth Redman, 'what will you now that I shall do? I am your prisoner, ye have conquered me. I would gladly go again to Newcastle, and within fifteen days I shall come to you into Scotland, whereas ye shall assign me.' 'I am content,' quoth Lindsay: 'ye shall promise by your faith to present yourself within this three weeks at Edinboro, and wheresoever ye go, to repute yourself my prisoner.' All this sir Matthew sware and promised to fulfil. Then each of them took their horses and took leave each of other. Sir James returned, and his intent was to go to his own company the same way that he came, and sir Matthew Redman to Newcastle.

Sir James Lindsay could not keep the right way as he came: it was dark and a mist, and he had not ridden half a mile, but he met face to face with the bishop of Durham and more than five hundred Englishmen with him. He might well escaped if he had would, but he supposed it had been his own company, that had pursued the Englishmen. When he was among them, one demanded of him what he was. 'I am,' quoth he, 'sir James Lindsay.' The bishop heard those words and stept to him and said: 'Lindsay, ye are taken: yield ye to me.' 'Who be you?' quoth Lindsay. 'I am,' quoth he, 'the bishop of Durham.' 'And from whence come you, sir?' quoth Lindsay. 'I come from the battle,' quoth the bishop, 'but I struck never a stroke there: I go back to Newcastle for this night, and ye shall go with me.' 'I may not choose,' quoth Lindsay, 'sith ye will have it so. I have taken and I am taken; such is the adventures of arms.' 'Whom have ye taken?' quoth the bishop. 'Sir,' quoth he, 'I took in the chase sir Matthew Redman.' 'And where is he?' quoth the bishop. 'By my faith, sir, he is returned to Newcastle: he desired me to trust him on his faith for three weeks, and so have I done.' 'Well,' quoth the bishop, 'let us go to Newcastle, and there ye shall speak with him.' Thus they rode to Newcastle together, and sir James Lindsay was prisoner to the bishop of Durham.

Under the banner of the earl de la March and of Dunbar was taken a squire of Gascoyne, called John of Chateauneuf, and under the banner of the earl of Moray was taken his companion John de Cantiron. Thus the field was clean avoided, or the day appeared. The Scots drew together and took guides and sent out scurrers to see if any men were in the way from Newcastle, to the intent that they would not be troubled in their lodgings; wherein they did wisely, for when the bishop of Durham was come again to Newcastle and in his lodging, he was sore pensive and wist not what to say nor do; for he heard say how his cousins the Percies were slain or taken, and all the knights that were with them. Then he sent for all the knights and squires that were in the town; and when they were come, he demanded of them if they should leave the matter in that case, and said: 'Sirs, we shall bear great blame if we thus return without looking on our enemies.' Then they concluded by the sun-rising every man to be armed, and on horseback and afoot to depart out of the town and to go to Otterburn to fight with the Scots. This was warned through the town by a trumpet, and every man armed them and assembled before the bridge, and by the sun-rising they departed by the gate towards Berwick and took the way towards Otterburn to the number of ten thousand, what afoot and a-horseback. They were not gone past two mile from Newcastle, when the Scots were signified that the bishop of Durham was coming to themward to fight: this they knew by their spies, such as they had set in the fields.

After that sir Matthew Redman was returned to Newcastle and had shewed to divers how he had been taken prisoner by sir James Lindsay, then it was shewed him how the

The Battle of Otterburn

bishop of Durham had taken the said sir James Lindsay and how that he was there in the town as his prisoner. As soon as the bishop was departed, sir Matthew Redman went to the bishop's lodging to see his master, and there he found him in a study, lying in a window[†] and said: 'What, sir James Lindsay, what make you here?' Then sir James came forth of the study to him and gave him good morrow, and said: 'By my faith, sir Matthew, fortune hath brought me hither; for as soon as I was departed from you, I met by chance the bishop of Durham, to whom I am prisoner, as ye be to me. I believe ye shall not need to come to Edinboro to me to make your finance: I think rather we shall make an exchange one for another, if the bishop be so content.' 'Well, sir,' quoth Redman, 'we shall accord right well together, ye shall dine this day with me: the bishop and our men be gone forth to fight with your men, I cannot tell what shall fall, we shall know at their return.' 'I am content to dine with you,' quoth Lindsay. Thus these two knights dined together in Newcastle.

When the knights of Scotland were informed how the bishop of Durham came on them with ten thousand men, they drew to council to see what was best for them to do, other to depart or else to abide the adventure. All things considered, they concluded to abide, for they said they could not be in a better nor a stronger place than they were in already: they had many prisoners and they could not carry them away, if they should have departed; and also they had many of their men hurt and also some of their prisoners, whom they thought they would not leave behind them. Thus they drew together and ordered so their field, that there was no entry but one way, and they set all their prisoners together and made them to promise how that, rescue or no rescue, they should be their prisoners. After that they made all their minstrels to blow up all at once and made the greatest

---

[†] Or rather, 'very pensive leaning against a window,' and afterwards the expression 'came forth of the study to him' should be 'broke off his thought and came towards him.'

revel of the world. Lightly it is the usage of Scots, that when they be thus assembled together in arms, the footmen beareth about their necks horns in manner like hunters, some great, some small, and of all sorts, so that when they blow all at once, they make such a noise, that it may be heard nigh four miles off: thus they do to abash their enemies and to rejoice themselves. When the bishop of Durham with his banner and ten thousand men with him were approached within a league, then the Scots blew their horns in such wise, that it seemed that all the devils in hell had been among them, so that such as heard them and knew not of their usage were sore abashed. This blowing and noise endured a long space and then ceased: and by that time the Englishmen were within less than a mile. Then the Scots began to blow again and made a great noise, and as long endured as it did before. Then the bishop approached with his battle well ranged in good order and came within the sight of the Scots, as within two bow-shot or less: then the Scots blew again their horns a long space. The bishop stood still to see what the Scots would do and aviewed them well and saw how they were in a strong ground greatly to their advantage. Then the bishop took counsel what was best for him to do; but all things well advised, they were not in purpose to enter in among the Scots to assail them, but returned without doing of anything, for they saw well they might rather lose than win.

When the Scots saw the Englishmen recule and that they should have no battle, they went to their lodgings and made merry, and then ordained to depart from thence. And because that sir Ralph Percy was sore hurt, he desired of his master that he might return to Newcastle or into some place, whereas it pleased him, unto such time as he were whole of his hurts, promising, as soon as he were able to ride, to return into Scotland, other to Edinboro or into any other place appointed. The earl of March, under whom he was taken, agreed thereto and delivered him a horse litter and sent him away; and by like covenant divers other knights and squires were suffered to return and took term other to return or else to pay their finance, such as

The Battle of Otterburn

they were appointed unto. It was shewed me by the information of the Scots, such as had been at this said battle that was between Newcastle and Otterburn in the year of our Lord God a thousand three hundred fourscore and eight, the nineteenth day of August, how that there were taken prisoners of the English party a thousand and forty men, one and other, and slain in the field and in the chase eighteen hundred and forty, and sore hurt more than a thousand: and of the Scots there were a hundred slain, and taken in the chase more than two hundred; for as the Englishmen fled, when they saw any advantage they returned again and fought: by that means the Scots were taken and none otherwise. Every man may well consider that it was a well fought field, when there were so many slain and taken on both parties.

How the Scots departed and carried with them the Earl Douglas dead, and buried him in the Abbey of Melrose; and how Sir Archambault Douglas and his company departed from before Carlisle and returned into Scotland

AFTER this battle thus finished, every man returned,[*] and the earl Douglas' dead body chested and laid in a chare, and with him sir Robert Hart and Simon Glendowyn, then they prepared to depart: so they departed and led with them sir Henry Percy and more than forty knights of England, and took the way to the abbey of Melrose. At their departing they set fire in their lodgings, and rode all the day, and yet lay that night in the English ground: none denied them. The next day they dislodged early in the morning and so came that day to Melrose. It is an abbey of black monks on the border between both realms. There they rested and buried the earl James Douglas. The second day after his obsequy was done reverently, and on his body laid a tomb of stone and his banner hanging over him. Whether there were as then any more earls of Douglas, to whom the land returned, or not, I cannot tell; for I, sir John Froissart, author of this book, was in Scotland in the earl's castle of Dalkeith, living earl William, at which time he had two children, a son and a

---

[*] That is, 'After the battle was over and every man had returned,' but it should be, 'After all this was done and everything was gathered together.'

The Battle of Otterburn

daughter; but after there were many of the Douglases, for I have seen a five brethren, all squires, bearing the name of Douglas, in the king of Scotland's house, David; they were sons to a knight in Scotland called sir James Douglas, and they bare in their arms gold, three oreilles[†] gules, but as for the heritage, I know not who had it: as for sir Archambault Douglas, of whom I have spoken before in this history in divers places, who was a valiant knight, and greatly redoubted of the Englishmen, he was but a bastard.

When these Scots had been at Melrose abbey and done there all that they came thither for, then they departed each from other and went into their own countries, and such as had prisoners, some led them away with them and some were ransomed and suffered to return. Thus the Englishmen found the Scots right courteous and gentle in their deliverance and ransom, so that they were well content. This was shewed me in the country of Bearn in the earl of Foix's house by a knight named John of Chateauneuf, who was taken prisoner at the same journey under the banner of the earl of March and Dunbar: and he greatly praised the said earl, for he suffered him to pass in manner as he desired himself.

Thus these men of war of Scotland departed, and ransomed their prisoners as soon as they might right courteously, and so returned little and little into their own countries. And it was shewed me and I believe it well, that the Scots had by reason of that journey two hundred thousand franks for ransoming of prisoners: for sith the battle that was before Stirling in Scotland, whereas sir Robert of Bruce, sir William Douglas, sir Robert Versy, sir Simon Fraser and other Scots chased the Englishmen three days, they never had journey so profitable nor so honourable for them, as this was. When tidings came to the other company of the Scots that were beside Carlisle, how their company had distressed the Englishmen

---

[†] Oreilles = ears.

beside Otterburn, they were greatly rejoiced, and displeased in their minds that they had not been there. Then they determined to dislodge and to draw into their own countries, seeing their other company were withdrawn. Thus they dislodged and entered into Scotland.

Now let us leave to speak of the Scots and of the Englishmen for this time, and let us return to the young Charles of France, who with a great people went into Almaine, to bring the duke of Gueldres to reason.

When the French king and all his army were past the river of Meuse at the bridge of Morsay, they took the way of Ardennes and of Luxembourg, and always the pioneers were before, beating woods and bushes and making the ways plain. The duke of Juliers and his country greatly doubted the coming of the French king, for they knew well they should have the first assault and bear the first burden: and the land of Juliers is a plain country; in one day the men of war should do much damage there, and destroy and waste all, except the castles and good towns. Thus the French king entered into the country of Luxembourg and came to an abbey, whereas Wenceslas sometime duke of Brabant was buried. There the king tarried two days: then he departed and took the way through Bastogne, and lodged within a league whereas the duchess of Brabant lay. She sent word of her being there to the duke of Burgoyne, and he brought her into the field to speak with the king, who received her right honourably, and there communed together. Then the duchess returned to Bastogne, and thither she was conveyed with sir John of Vienne and sir Guy of Tremouille; and the next day the king went forward, approaching to the land of his enemies, and came to the entering into Almaine, on the frontiers of the duchy of Juliers. But or he came so far forward, Arnold bishop of Liege had been with the king and had greatly entreated for the duke of Juliers, that the king should not be miscontent with him, though he were father to the duke of Gueldres; for he excused him of the defiance that his son had

The Battle of Otterburn

made, affirming how it was not by his knowledge nor consent, wherefore, he said, it were pity that the father should bear the default of the son. His excuse was not sufficient to the king nor to his uncles: for the intent of the king and his council was, without the duke of Juliers would come and make other manner of excuse, and to yield himself to the king's pleasure, his country should be the first that should bear the burden. Then the bishop of Liege and the lords of Hesbaing and the councils of the good towns offered to the king and his council wholly the bishopric of Liege for his army to pass and repass paying for their expenses, and to rest and refresh them there as long as it pleased them. The king thanked them, and so did his uncles, and would not refuse their offer, for he knew not what need he should have after.

Index

N.B. Individuals are generally listed by their first name, lords by their title.

Abbeville, 24, 26, 27, 28, 32, 33, 40
Acier, Lord of, 65
Acon, Lord of, 65
Agace, Gobin, 26, 28
Aiguillon, 7, 8
Airaines, 22, 23, 24, 27
Alençon, Earl of, 34, 36, 38, 53, 64
Alexander Ramsay, Sir, 130
Almaine, 8, 13, 36, 60, 142
Alnwick, 116, 118
Amboise, 47
Amery of Tastes, Lord, 64
Amiens, 19, 20, 23, 24, 26, 39
Amposte, Chatelain of, 57, 63, 82
Anjou, 47, 48
Archambault Douglas, Sir, 131, 141
Archers, 7, 10, 14, 16, 18, 20, 23, 27, 31, 34, 35, 37, 40, 52, 53, 56, 57, 60, 61, 62, 63, 69, 124
Ardennes, 142
Argenton, Lord, 64
Arnold d'Audrehem, Lord, 51, 61
Arnold of Cervolles, Lord, 53, 64
Arnold of Rayneval, Lord, 65
Artois
  Men of, 27
Artois, Lord Robert of, 28
Arundel, 106
Arundel, Earl of, 8, 10, 31, 34, 96
Athens, Duke of, 51, 63, 64, 65
Aubigny, Lord of, 32, 39
Aumale, Countess of, 28
Aumale, Earl of, 38
Aunay, Earl of, 64
Austreham. *See* Ouistreham
Auxerre, Earl of, 39

Avignon, 123
Aymenion of Pommiers, Sir, 49

Ball, John. *See* John Ball
Barfleur, 10
Bartholmew of Burghersh, Lord, 8, 30, 49, 57, 70, 77
Basset, Lord, 8, 22, 31, 57
Bastogne, 142
Baudrin de la Heuse, Sir, 65
Bazeilles, Moine of, 32
Beaujeu, Lord of, 32, 39
Beauvais, 21, 40
Beauvoir, 69
Beauvoisis, 21
Bedfordshire, 87, 90, 92, 93, 103, 106
Berkeley, Lord, 8, 57, 67, 68
Bernard of Truttes, 82
Berry, 48
Berwick-upon-Tweed, 116, 130, 136
Blackheath, 94
Blanche-taque, 25
  Battle of, 26–29
Blangy, 43
Blaye, 81
Blois, 47
Blois, Earl of, 1, 20, 38
Bordeaux, 75, 80, 81, 82
Boulogne, 43
Boulogne (Paris), 20
Bourbon
  Knights of, 64

Bourbon, Duke of, 51, 64, 65
Bourchier, Lord, 30
Bourg-la-Reine, 20
Brabant, Duchess of, 142
Bradestan, Lord of, 8
Bradetane, Lord, 57
Bretayne (Brittany), 9
Brosse, Viscount of, 49
Broye, 37
  Castle of, 39
Buch, Captal of, 49, 57, 64, 69, 82
Burgoyne, Duke of, 47, 142

Caen, 9, 15, 19
  Battle of, 16–18
Calais, 17, 43
Cambridgeshire, 96, 103, 106
Canterbury, 91, 92
Canterbury, Archbishop of, 7, 88, 89, 91, 94, 101
Carentan, 11
Carlisle, 115, 118, 131, 140, 141
Cavalry, 26, 28, 32, 37, 48, 50, 57, 132, 136
Chalons, Bishop of, 65
Chamy, Lord of, 70
Charles Duke of Normandy, 47
Charles II, King of Navarre, 47
Charles of Montmorency, Sir, 39

Index

Charles V, King of France, 142
Charles, Prince of Bohemia, 13, 36
Chartres, 47, 52
Châtellerault, 48, 68
Chatillon, Lord, 51
Chauny, Lord of, 65
Chauvigny, 48, 63, 80
Chauvigny, Lord of, 49
Cherbourg, 11
Chivalry, 2, 54
Clarence, Duke of, 1
Clermont, Lord, 51, 56
Condon, Lord of, 57
Coppegueule, 23
Corbie, 22
Cornwall, 8
Cornwall, Earl of, 8
Corpus Christi, Feast of, 92, 97, 103
Cotentin, Isle of, 9, 12
Coutances, 14
Craon, Lord of, 48
Crecy (Cressy), 28
  Battle of, 34–39
    Aftermath, 40–41, 42–43
    Preparations for, 30–31, 32–33
Creuse, River, 48
Crotoy, 26, 28
Currours (Cavalry), 27
Currours (light cavalrymen), 26

Dalkeith, 117, 123, 140

Dammartin, Earl of, 51, 64, 69, 79
Daniel Pasele, Lord, 58
Dargies, 21
Davie Collemine, 127
Delaware, Lord, 8, 30, 57
Denis of Morbeke, Lord, 58, 70, 71, 82
Douglas, Earl of, 65, 96, 115–19, 122, 124–25, 126–28
  Death of, 140
Dreux, Earl of, 19
Dunbar, Earl of, 115, 125, 128, 136, 141
Duras, Sir Robert, 51
Durham, 106, 116
  Bishopric of, 115, 132
Durham, Bishop of, 7, 120, 121, 131, 132, 134–39

Edmund of Alphel, Sir, 117, 120
Edward III, King of England, 1, 7, 9, 10, 13, 14, 15, 19, 20, 23, 24, 26–29, 30–31, 34–39, 42, 70, 82
Edward, the Black Prince, 1, 7, 8, 14, 30, 59–66, 70, 73
England
  Commons of, 92–96, 94, 96, 102
  Nobles of, 93, 96, 101, 102
Englishmen

As fighters, 22, 41, 123, 130
Order of battle, 14, 30–31, 34
Essex, 87, 90, 92, 93, 103, 106
Eustace of Ribemont, Lord, 65
Eustace, Lord of Aubrecicourt, 48, 49, 58, 60
Evreux, 19

Felton, Lord of, 8, 57
Fenton, Lord of, 130
Fiennes, Lord, 51
Fife, Earl of, 131
Fitz-Warin, Lord, 8
Flanders, Earl of, 13, 20, 36, 38
Foix, Earl of, 122, 141
Frenchmen
As fighters, 27
Order of battle, 32–33, 34, 51

Gascony, 7, 8, 9, 82, 136
Men of, 64, 70, 75
Genoese, 15, 26, 27, 34–39
Geoffrey Chaucer, 2
Geoffrey of Charny, Lord, 51, 70
Geoffrey of Saint-Dizier, Lord, 65
Gironde, River, 81
Godemar du Fay, Sir, 26–29

Godfrey of Harcourt, 7, 9, 10, 12, 16, 17, 19, 20, 30, 38
Gommegnies, Lord of, 91, 94, 101, 102
Grandvilliers, 21
Grismouton of Chambly, Sir, 65
Gueldres, Duke of, 142
Guichard d'Angle, Lord, 63, 64, 69
Guichard of Beaujeu, Lord, 65
Guildford, 106
Guilliam Lister of Stafford, 103, 106
Guines, Earl of, 9, 15
Guy of Tremouille, Sir, 142
Guy Stuart, Sir, 130

Hainault, Earl of, 8
Hainault, Lord John of, 13, 20, 27, 33, 37, 39
Hampton, 96
Hangest, Lord of, 65
Harcourt Earl of, 19
Helly, Lord of, 65
Helton, Baron of, 130
Henry Percy, Sir, 116, 117, 118, 119, 120, 121, 122, 129, 140
Hereford, Earl of, 8
Hesbaing, 143
Hesdin, 43
Hilton, Baron of, 116
Hogue Saint-Vaast, 9, 10
Holland, Sir John, 94, 102

148

Index

Holland, Sir Thomas, 12, 17, 18, 22
Hundred Years' War, 1
Huntingdon, Earl of, 8, 10, 15, 18

Infantry, 7, 14, 26, 32, 52, 54, 121, 130, 132, 136, 138
Innocent the Sixth, Pope, 47
Irishmen, 7

Jack Straw, 90, 92, 98, 101, 103, 105, 111
James Audley, Sir, 8, 57, 59, 60, 61, 65, 73–74, 77–78, 81
James d'Artois, Lord, 64
James Earl of Douglas. *See* Douglas, Earl of
James of Beaujeu, Lord, 64
James of Bourbon, Lord, 64, 79
Jaques of Bourbon, Lord, 51, 69
Jean Froissart, 1, 140
Jean Lebel, 2
John Ball, 89, 90, 92, 98, 101, 103, 105, 111
  Sermon of, 88
John Chandos, Sir, 8, 22, 30, 56, 59, 61, 62, 63, 71
John Clermont, Lord, 61
John Coppledike, Sir, 116
John d'Artois, Lord, 64, 79
John Felton, Sir, 116
John Haliburton, Sir, 130

John II, King of France, 47–50, 51–53, 54–58, 59–66, 69–72
John Lilleburn, Sir, 116, 130
John Maxwell, Sir, 130
John Newton, Sir, 93, 94, 95, 97
John of Artois, Lord, 69
John of Cantiron, 122
John of Caumont, Lord, 57
John of Chateauneuf, 122, 136, 141
John of Colpedich, Sir, 130
John of Ghistelles, Lord, 48, 58
John of Hellenes, 67
John of Landas, Lord, 51, 52, 63, 64
John of Normandy, 52
John of Saint-Moreaulx, Sir, 130
John of Saintre, Lord, 63, 64, 69
John of Vienne, Sir, 142
John Sinclair, Sir, 127, 128
John Standish, Sir, 108, 109
John Tycle, 106
John, Duke of Berry, 47
John, King of Bohemia, 13, 20, 27, 32, 36
John, Louis and Roger of Beauchamp, Sirs, 8
Joigny, Earl of, 48, 49
Joinville, Earl of, 65, 79
Juliers, Duke of, 142

Kent, 87, 88, 90, 91, 103

Kent, Earl of, 7, 94, 102
King of Bohemia. *See* John, King of Bohemia
King of England. *See* Edward III and Richard II
King of France. *See* Philip VI, John II and Charles V
King of Navarre. *See* Charles II
King's Lynn, 103, 106

La Haye en Touraine, 47
La Tour, Lord of, 64, 65
Lancaster, Duke of, 96, 98, 101, 103
Landas, Lord of, 53, 65
Landiras, Lord of, 58
Languiran, Lord of, 57, 64
Lascelles, Lord, 31
Latimer, Lord of, 30
Latrau, Lord of, 64
Lesparre, Lord of, 57
Liege, Bishop of, 142
Lincoln, Bishop of, 7
Lincolnshire, 14, 93, 106
Lindsay, Sir William, James and Alexander, 130
Linieres, Lord of, 64
Loches, 47
Loire, River, 47
Lombards, 99
London, 90, 106
  Aldermen, 109
  Mayor of, 90, 94, 99, 108, 109
  Tower of, 91, 94, 97, 98, 99, 100
London Bridge, 101
Long-en-Ponthieu, 23
Longpre, 23
Lorraine, Duke of, 13, 20, 38
Louis of Melval, Sir, 65
Louis of Normandy, 52
Louis of Recombes, Lord, 60
Louis Tufton, Sir, 31
Louis, Duke of Anjou, 47
Lucy, Lord, 8, 31, 132
Luxembourg, 142

Manne, Lord, 57
Manne, Lord of, 8
Mantes, 19
Marc Adreman, Sir, 130
March, Earl of, 8, 115, 125, 128, 136, 138, 141
Mareuil, Lord of, 65
Marshalsea Prison, 98
Matthew Redman, Sir, 116, 130, 134, 135, 136, 137
Maupertuis, 69, 75
Melrose, Abbey of, 140
Melval, Lord of, 65
Men of arms, 7, 10, 12, 13, 14, 18, 20, 23, 26, 30, 31, 34, 35, 36, 37, 47, 48, 49, 51, 52, 53, 57, 61, 62, 71, 80
Mercoeur, Lord of, 64
Meulan, 19
Meung, 47
Meuse, River, 142
Mile-end, 100, 102

Index

Milly, 21
Mohun, Lord of, 30
Mons, Earl of, 65
Montaigu, Lord of, 64
Montebourg, 11
Montendre, Lord of, 64, 69
Montferrand, Lord of, 58, 82
Montjoie, 20
Montreuil-sur-Mer, 43
Montsault, Lord of, 39, 65
Moorlane, 96
Moray, Earl of, 96, 115, 125, 126, 128, 131, 136
Morsay, Bridge of, 142
Mowbray, Lord of, 8
Moylays, Lord, 93
Multon, Lord of, 8, 31
Mussidan, Lord of, 64

Nassau, Earl of, 53, 60, 63
Nesle, Lord of, 51
Newcastle-upon-Tyne, 115–19, 120–23, 129–33, 134–39
Nicholas Bramber, Sir, 109
Nicholas Walworth, Sir, 99, 109
Nicholas, Cardinal of Urgel, 47
Nidau, Earl of, 53
Normandy, 8, 9, 12, 13, 15, 19, 26, 52, 57, 80
Normandy, Duke of, 61, 63
Northampton, Earl of, 8, 31, 34

Northumberland, Earl of, 117
Norwich, 103
Noyelles, 28
Noyers, Lord of, 32

Oisemont, 24, 26
Orléans, 52
    Bridge of, 47
Orléans, Duke of, 51, 52, 64
Otterburn, 120
    Battle of, 120–23, 124–25, 126–28, 129–33
    Castle of, 118
Oudart of Renty, Sir, 67
Ouistrehem (Austreham), 15, 18
Oxford, 106
Oxford, Earl of, 8, 30, 38, 57, 94, 97, 101

Palace of Westminster. *See* Royal, The
Paris, 1, 9, 20, 21, 52
Partenay, Lord of, 64, 69, 79
Pastoureaux, The, 90
Patrick of Dunbar, Sir, 130
Patrick of Hepbourn, Sir, 122
Peasant's Revolt, 87–91, 92–96, 97–101, 102–11
Percy, Henry de, 2nd Baron Percy, 7
Perducas d'Albret, Sir, 100, 109
Perigord, Cardinal of, 47, 54–58, 62, 82

Peter Audley, Sir, 8, 57, 77
Philip VI, King of France, 9, 13, 17, 20, 21, 23, 26, 27, 32–33, 34–39
Philip, Duke of Burgoyne, 47
Philippa of Hainault, Queen, 1
Picardy
  Knights of, 64
  Men of, 27
Picquigny, 23
Pierrebuffiere, Lord of, 65
Poissy, 16, 19, 20
Poitiers, 48, 49
  Battle of, 59–66
    Aftermath, 67–68, 69–72, 75–76, 77–78, 79, 80–83
    Negotiations before, 54–58
    Preparations for, 47–50, 51–53
  Men of, 64
Poitiers, Earl of, 63
Poitou, 47, 81
  Wines of, 28
Poix, 22
Pommiers, Lord of, 57, 64
Pompadour, Lord of, 65, 70
Pons, Lord of, 64, 69
Pont-a-Remy, 23
Pont-de-l'Arche, 19
Ponthieu, Earl of, 51, 69
Pontland, 115, 117, 120
Prince of Wales. *See* Edward the Black Prince

Prisoners of war, 17, 19, 24, 36, 49, 55, 63, 65, 69, 71, 78, 79, 80, 131, 137, 139, 141
Ransoms, 75, 82, 141

Queen's Wardrobe, The, 101

Ralph Lumley, Sir, 116, 130
Ralph Neville, Baron, 7
Ralph Percy, Sir, 116, 119
Raoul, Lord of Coucy, 48
Rauzan, Lord of, 57
Raynold Cobham, Sir, 8, 12, 22, 30, 38, 42, 57, 70, 71, 73, 74
Reading, 106
Ribemont, Lord Eustace, 51, 52
Richard II, King of England, 102, 105
Richard Lyon, 99
Richard of Beaujeu, Lord, 52
Richard of Pembridge, Sir, 8
Richard of Pembroke, Lord, 57
Robert Collemine, Sir, 130
Robert Hart, 140
Robert Hart, Sir, 127
Robert Knolles, Sir, 100, 109
Robert Nevill, Sir, 30
Robert of Bruce, Sir, 141
Robert of Duras, Lord, 62

Index

Robert of Namur, Sir, 91, 94, 101
Robert Ogle, Sir, 116
Robert Sale, Sir, 104, 105
Robert Versy, Sir, 141
Rochechouart, Viscount of, 64
Rochelle
  Merchants of, 28
Rochester, Kent, 92
Rochfort, Lord of, 64
Roger of Wetenhale, Sir, 8
Rolleboise, 19
Romorantin
  Castle of, 47
Ros, Lord, 8, 31
Rouen, 19, 40
  Archbishop of, 41
Roxburgh, 96
Royal, The (Palace of Westminster), 103
  Queen's Wardrobe, 105, 110

Saint Andrew, Abbey of, 81
Saint John's Hospital, 98
Saint Katherine's, 99
Saint Peter, Abbey of, 32
Saint Thomas, Church of, Canterbury, 92
Saint Vincent, Abbey of, 92
Saint-Aubin, Lord of, 31
Saint-Cloud, 20
Saint-Denis, 20, 23
Saint-Germain-en-Laye, 20
Saint-Lô, 12, 14
Saint-Messie, Abbey of, 21

Saintonge, 81
  Merchants of, 28
Saint-Pol, Earl of, 39
Saint-Riquier, 26, 27, 40
Saint-Sauveur-le-Vicomte, 9, 18
Saint-Valery, 24
Saint-Venant, Lord of, 51, 53, 64
Salisbury, Earl of, 57, 91, 94, 97, 100, 101, 110
Salm, Earl of, 13
Sarrebruck, Earl of, 13, 51, 53, 63
Saumur, 47
Savoy, Earl of, 29
Savoy, The, 98
Scots
  As fighters, 123, 124, 130
  Treaty with, 96
Seine, River, 16, 19
Serain, 43
Serignac, Lord of, 65
Simon Fraser, Sir, 141
Simon Glendowyn, 131, 140
Sinclair, Sirs John and Walter, 130
Smithfield, 106, 109
Somme, River, 16, 22, 23, 24, 26, 27
Soudic of Latrau, Lord, 58
Spencer, Lord, 57
Stafford, Lord, 30
Stafford, Sir Richard, 42
Staffordshire, 103, 106
Stephen of Cosington, Lord, 57, 77

Stephen of Hales, Sir, 93
Stirling, 141
Straw, Jack. *See* Jack Straw
Suffolk, Earl of, 8, 12, 57, 64
Sully, Lord of, 51
Surgères, Lord of, 64
Sussex, 87, 90, 92, 93, 103, 106
Sutherland, Earl of, 96, 131

Tancarville, Earl of, 9, 15, 16, 18, 51, 69, 79
Tannay-Bouton, Lord of, 64
Thibault of Vaudenay, Lord, 53, 63
Thomas Abingdon, Sir, 116, 130
Thomas Baker, 106
Thomas Clifford,, 30
Thomas Erskine, Sir, 130
Thomas Gray, Sir, 130
Thomas Grey, Sir, 116
Thomas Helton, Sir, 130
Thomas Holland, Sir, 30
Thomas Holton, Sir, 116
Thomas of Cosington, Sir, 93
Thomas Ogle, Sir, 130
Thomas Versy, Earl, 96
Touraine, 47, 48, 63
Tours, 47, 48
Troyes, 29
Tyler, Wat. *See* Wat Tyler

Vaudenay, Lord of, 64, 65
Vaudimont, Earl of, 65

Vendome, Earl of, 65
Ventadour, Earl of, 51, 64
Vernon, 19
Vertaing, Lord of, 94, 101
Vimeu, 24

Waben, 43
Warin, Lord, 57
Warwick, Earl of, 8, 9, 10, 12, 30, 38, 57, 64, 71, 73, 74, 94, 97, 101
Warwickshire, 93, 106
Wat Tyler, 90, 92, 97–101, 102–11
Welshmen, 7, 31, 39
Westminster, 98, 105
William Douglas, Sir, 123, 141
William of Montaigu, Lord, 65
William of Namur, Earl, 13
William of Nesle, Lord, 65
William of North Berwick, 127
William Walsingham, Sir, 130
Willoughby, Lord, 8, 31, 57, 77
Winchester, 96
Wissant, 43
Wulfart of Ghistelles, Sir, 8

Yarmouth, 103, 104, 106
York, Archbishop of, 7
York, Seneschal of, 116, 130
Yorkshire, 106, 116

www.ingramcontent.com/pod-product-compliance
Lightning Source LLC
Chambersburg PA
CBHW031355040426
42444CB00005B/305